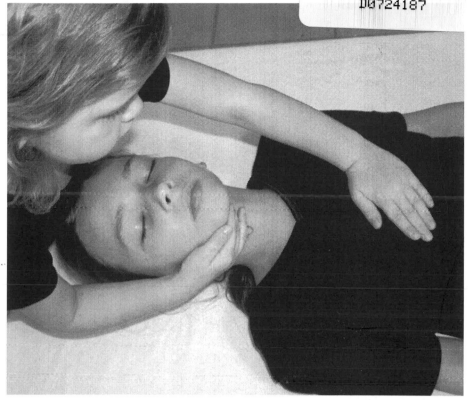

REIKI FOR CHILDREN

KYTKA HILMAR-JEZEK, ND

Reiki for Children
SECOND EDITION

Copyright © 2001 Kytka Hilmar-Jezek
Photographs © 2001 Kytka Hilmar-Jezek
Illustrations © 2001 Pavel Jezek
Reiki Symbol Graphics © Dennis Alexander

Book Cover Design by Kytka Hilmar-Jezek
Book Layout by Sunny DiMartino

Note to the Reader: This book is intended as an informational guide. The remedies, approaches, and techniques described herein are meant to supplement, and not to be a substitute for, professional medical care or treatment. They should not be used for a serious ailment without prior consultation with a qualified healthcare professional.

Printed in the U.S.A.

10 9 8 7 6 5 4 3 2 1

Library of Congress Cataloging-in-Publication Data

Hilmar-Jezek, Kytka 1964-
        Reiki Kids: Little Hands that Heal, A Reiki Manual for Children
        Includes Bibliographical References
        ISBN:9781453736906

Summary: A Manual introducing the healing art of Reiki to children.

1. Reiki. 2. Hands on Healing 3. Raw Foods 4. Family – Religious life. 5. Children – religious life. 6. Spiritual Exercises 7. Alternative Therapies 8. Children – spirituality. 9. Mind and Body

Family Healing Series
6822 – 22nd Avenue North, Suite 345
Saint Petersburg, Florida, 33710-3918

First published by Author House in 2001
Printed in the United States of America

www.FamilyHealingSeries.com

TABLE OF CONTENTS

ACKNOWLEDGMENTS

This Second Edition of the book is dedicated to my children,
Zachary, Zanna & Zynnia.
For they are the true teachers, gurus, mentors, leaders and wise ones.

It is also dedicated to Fabricio Andres Umana Solera
For teaching me the way of NOW and that
Love is indeed Cosmic, Multi-Dimensional and Eternal

May the warmth of the Divine Universal Light
Shine its goodness on you for your entire lives and beyond.

I am deeply grateful to all those who contributed their time, experience, creativity and wisdom to the creation of this book and for crossing paths with me in this life... many are listed in the bibliography section of this book.

In this second edition, I wish to acknowledge my dear friends and mentors who I would not be standing today without their love, kindness and intervention: Ballardo Zuniga, John Colandrea, Linda Burhans, Mario Hundertajlo, Gary King, Anil & Meena Gupta, Tony Robbins, Topher Morrison, Chris Krimitsos, Louie & Jini Pinto, Ivonne Delaflor, Louis Lautman, Joel Bauer, friends at TWBA Online, The Wealth Building Annex, Justin Fishman, Elliot Kay, Argentina, Phillip Black, Eric Voltz, Alban Morales Mena, Jeannette Reid, Donna Reiss, Renee Quinn, Georgia Abbate, Louise Hay, Big Wheel, Simone, and numerous other angels that have crossed my path – you know who you are and you continue to inspire me as you live in your lives in selfless acts of service. I also wish to acknowledge Costa Rica and the Corazon de Ticos, which without I would not be who I am today.

And, referring to the original edition, I wish to offer acknowledgement...

To my parents, Milan and Anna Hilmar, who instilled in me a "pioneer spirit" which has helped me to follow my own path. To Kati and Joel Samon, for giving us all shelter from the storm. To Informed Birth and Parenting, for starting me on the path of empowerment and belief in myself, including three absolute Goddesses: Leslie Stewart, Heike Doyle and Karin Kearns, all wise women and midwives who allow babies to come into this world in the most respectful ways, who were there to welcome my three angels into the world. To the wonderful people of Belize, whose traditional ways should never be forgotten. To my dear friends and Masters, Dennis and Fern Alexander, for gently appearing in my life at a time when I needed their guidance and welcoming us all into their circle. To my (now ex) husband, Pavel

Jezek, who has often been a quiet example of inner peace and balance, and whose continuing support and letting go allowed me to grow to who I am today.

To my children, the true teachers, gurus, mentors, leaders and wise ones.

To the Divine Light, which I see shining in everything and everyone I encounter—each and every day.

To the Darkness, because without it how would we ever know the Light.

And finally, to Steve who gave me the important lesson of overcoming obstacles, perseverance and forgiveness.

~ My life has indeed been blessed. ~

Namaste

FOREWORD

In today's uncertain world, children are our strength. It is within the child that our world and the Universe expands and grows. This book opens the door to the Universal Life Force, for those wonderful expansive minds of the youth of today.

Not every child is ready for the power of Reiki, those that are, shall benefit remarkably for the contents of this extraordinary work. What each child learns is a respect for the sacredness of Reiki. It aids them in connecting to the Universal Life Force, which is Universal Love.

Reiki teaches an individual: "Just for today, I will not worry, Just for today, I will not anger, Honor your parents, teachers and elders, earn your living honestly. Show gratitude to everything." Today when using the name of GOD in our own Pledge of Allegiance to our Flag is questioned, there must be an acceptable value which we may teach our children that circumvents the norm of dogma.

I plead you to reach out, touch our growing seeds, those which we planted and nurture them with the enlightened path of understanding, which will take their hands, open them to understanding and guide their paths to a higher good. One bereft of violence. It is our duty as parents, as leaders of people, to teach the little people how to become honorable big people. To whom the world will look to with RESPECT.

—*Rev. Dennis Alexander, PhD, Reiki Karuna Master,*
Mayan Shaman, K'in Balam XI Manik, Sentient Temple

X

FOREWORD
TO THE SECOND EDITION

Nearly ten years have passed since I wrote the book, Reiki For Children. It was written out of a necessity for my own children because I could not find any reference at that time to teach my children.

How wonderful it is to do research now and see so many new resources which give testament to the fact that our collective consciousness is catching on. Holistic methods are gaining popularity and becoming more mainstream and as a culture, we are beginning to understand the importance of taking responsibility for our own healing and wellness.

My children have grown up with no major illnesses, always referring back to Reiki to help each other and themselves. They eat correctly, meditate, focus on stress free living and teach others to do the same.

I am very proud of who they are as BE-ings and proud of myself that I do not push them into doing. They walk their own free path and create wonders everywhere they go and each and every day.

They are a daily reminder that sometimes we may be afraid to try something that is off the beaten path or not the status quo, but of we feel it within and believe – then we can truly achieve anything. It is in parenting these three amazing human beings in who I am in awe daily that my life has prepared me for the challenges along the way.

Family and health are truly everything, and it is my intention to empower others to do the same by living by example.

—*Kytka Hilmar-Jezek*

WHO HAS THE HEALING TOUCH?

You do!

Did you know that you were born with incredible healing power?

Yes, you were.

It is a gift to you from the Mother Father Creator of All.

You were born out of Love.

You were born out of Light.

People call this very special and strong love Universal Life Force (or energy).

This powerful energy stays within you your whole life.

With this energy you can do anything you hope to do.

With practice, you can use this energy to heal.

But first you have to realize and believe that you have it. You can find it within yourself by taking the time to look and listen within. In the olden days, people would sit in nature and be still and quiet. They would meditate. During the still and quiet times as these, they would listen to their inner voices, which spoke loudly to them. Today we live in very busy and noisy times. It is hard to find a quiet place or to make quiet time... but this time is very important if we want to find our voices within and remember our light and its power.

REMEMBERING THE POWER

Long, long ago, before you were born, you were part of a beautiful and brilliant light. The light and its beauty were all around you and everyone glowed with this light. Many people call this the place of angels or heaven. Long ago, before you were born, this is where you lived. You probably cannot remember this place anymore in your mind, but your heart always remembers this place. You heart remembers the warmth and lightness of this place.

This place is always a part of you and still alive in your heart.

When you were first born, you remembered this place very well. It was hard to separate your new home from your old home in the light. You loved your parents, but you also loved the light beings that would always be around you, warming you with love. You wanted to tell every one of the love and beauty, but the only sounds that came out of your mouth were cries. This made you sad and your heart grew heavy. The heavier your heart became, the more the light began to hide deep inside of you.

Have you ever looked at a baby and seen how very knowing the baby looks. This is because the baby fully remembers all about this light place and can still see and feel all of the angels and other light beings all around. Babies have just come from this place and have not yet forgotten. Have you ever seen a baby laying down reaching out to the sun. The baby is probably holding one of her angels' hands at that very moment!

By the time you learned to speak enough words to tell people about the light, you had almost forgotten all about it. Sometimes the warm sun would shine its light down on you and you would feel so good, and warm, and you loved the sunlight... but you couldn't remember why.

As you grew older, your thoughts became like the thoughts of all of the other people around you. Mostly heavy thoughts of worries and of all that needed to be done: attending school, playing, eating, bathing.... These things do need to be tended to, but you must take time to remember the light. When you don't you become taken over with heavy thoughts and heavy thoughts are dark thoughts, they make you forget the light even quicker!

Many people in the world have been so busy that they forgot to take the time to remember. They have forgotten how important it is to remember the light. These folks have allowed these dark thoughts into them and they have become mean.

When you remember your light and try to do good and kind things, people who have forgotten their light may even make fun of you or call you names. Please do not let this make you turn away from the light. Try to send love to those people, because if they are being mean it only means they have forgotten their own light. They must be so sad and they do not even remember why. It is this sadness that causes them to be mean. Try to look at them with love, goodness and healing.

The most important thing you can do for yourself is to try and practice remembering the light from where you came.

You are a full of goodness.
You are full of loving kindness.
You have the power to help and heal others.

Remember that many people walk around with sad and angry faces because they have forgotten their light. They have heavy hearts and are unhappy. You have the power to help them remember their light too!

There are many people who spend their whole lives walking in the light spreading goodness and loving kindness all over the world. These people make our world a better and safer place. They make it a more peaceful and loving place. They make it become a world we are happy to live in. You can be one of these people!

You ARE one of these people!

Don't be worried if you cannot remember your light right now. You will soon. If you do the exercises in this book, you will soon remember. You will be able to use this light to help yourself and others. You will be filled with goodness, loving kindness and healing power. This light is much bigger than your room, your house, your neighborhood, your town, your world! This is the Universal Light Force and it is everything. You are a part of this very strong everything.

You are an important part of something great!

If you choose to follow the path of goodness and light, of love and healing you must be willing to work hard. You must learn to listen to your dreams, your inner voices, your spirit guides, your angels. You must look very deep into your body and soul to find your true power.

"Let your light shine before men, that they may see your good works."

"A tree does not move unless there is wind"

PLACES OF POWER.

A very good place for remembering the light is in nature.

The best start is to find a special and sacred place for yourself where you can work on your power. The best place is outside in nature, under the vast skies, where the sun and moon can touch your cheek, where the wind can whisper into your ear. Grandfather tree sees the light in you and if you sit with him, he may help you to remember. The wind sees the light and if you stand in the wind, maybe he will whisper of it into your ear. Mother moon looks down on you, calling you to look to the stars to remember. And don't forget the mighty Father Sun, his warmth can always remind you of how wonderful it is to be in the light.

Sit in nature every day and listen.
Soon you will feel the light again.
It is always with you.

The light is your inner voice, and it is your source of power. Use this light to help yourself. Use it to help other people. When someone is mean to you, it is because they have forgotten their light and their goodness. You can send them some of yours. You never run out... as a matter of fact, the more you are aware of it and use it, the more power you have.

The Universal Life Force energy never runs out. It keeps going around and around, encircling you and filling you with love, goodness and light. Look at mean and sad people with love and understanding and it may help them to remember. Some of your light may spread to them and it may help them to find their own light and listen to their own loving kindness and goodness.

Your power is strong and it lives within and around you.
You have the ability to use this power.

Many people have learned that everything is related and connected to each other. We are connected to the trees, and the animals that share this planet with us. We are a part of nature. Wisdom keepers of today warn us that if we become too disconnected from the natural world, we will forget the light all together and we will perish. We need to be close to the earth and nature because we are a part of it.

Outside we can breathe deeply and bury our toes in the soft sand or grass. We can smell the trees and flowers carried on the wind. We are reminded that there is so much in life that is beautiful and that everything has an important part of the planet. Each and every ant, bug, butterfly, flower, tree, river has a reason. These things were here long before us and they hold many answers. Listen to them.

Much like having dreams (the inner voices speaking to us in our sleep), listening to nature can provide answers to our questions and guide us on our way. Native Americans consulted nature each and every day. People of long ago prayed outside to the heavens... to the moon and the sun, long before there were churches and temples built.

People of the past worshiped the sun, because they felt it to be the source of all life. These people were very smart and understood the power of the Universal Life Force! On the earth, there are many ways and places where we can connect with this powerful energy. When we travel or take a holiday we often seek out places where the sun shines, or where there is great natural beauty. We are drawn and attracted to places where the elements of nature are felt, the mountains, the sea, the forests. These places seem to replenish OUR energies and make us feel good.

When you have a question or need comfort, go outside. Listen to the wind. Let the breeze encircle you because you are a part of the wind. You are a part of the outside world. You are a part of nature and it will comfort you.

You have a sacred place in nature.

You have a place in the circle of life.

Can you remember?

You have to WANT to remember.

You have to take TIME to remember.

TIME IS POWER.

The first step in learning about yourself and your power is to make time each and every day to listen within. This is the time when you work on yourself. This time is very important. It is with this time that your power will grow. It is the time you will exercise and grow your healing touch.

At first you may find you are just sitting and nothing is happening, but that is only because you have forgotten to listen to the voice within. When you were a small baby it spoke to you all the time. It helped you to smile and to stand tall. It helped you to walk and to learn to talk. It is inside of you still, but you learned to listen to Mom and Dad, Grandma and Grandpa and have forgotten to listen to the voice within.

If you sit in a quiet place everyday, soon you will remember and you will hear it once again.

This voice is the voice within your heart.
This voice is your guide, it is your teacher.
This voice is the voice of your Sacred Wisdom.

It is the same voice that spoke to your grandparents, and their parents, and their parents...

It is the voice of the Sacred Wisdom,
and Sacred Wisdom is power.

It is a power you can tap into at any moment, any where, any time. This power lets us be brave, be strong, be wise. We hear and feel this wisdom when we breathe deeply.

BREATH IS POWER.

When you sit, make sure to sit tall and proud. Imagine yourself sitting on the tallest mountain. Imagine your lower back is planted into the ground, like the roots of a tree and that on your head you wear a crown, which sparkles so brightly it touches the stars in the heavens. Rest your mouth and breathe in through your nose and out through your mouth. Breathe slowly and deeply.

The Zuni Indians believe that the human spirit lives in the breath. Bear Medicine Woman says "to breathe means to show power," and the bible calls breath, "the breath of life." Many people believe that our breath is a gift from the Mother Father Creator of All and when we die, we return this gift to the Universe where it once again becomes a part of the all.

Sitting and breathing like this, being still and quiet is called meditation.

Meditation is when you allow the mind to rest and go quiet. When you meditate you are opening yourself up to the goodness of the universe. You are listening deep within. You are connecting to the energy that is all around. This energy has great power, and is known as the Universal Life Force. You can open yourself up to this energy and allow it to share its power with you. You can use this time to let go of hurt or angry feelings, to stop being mad and to think of the goodness, which is inside you. You can use this time to invite more goodness to come and be inside you.

When we stop thinking about our every day activities and what keeps us busy, we begin to listen what is going on inside our selves. We begin to be able to hear our inner voice. We learn to listen to our body and what it has to say to us. If something is not right, our body tells us right away. We are able to talk to our body and tell it what needs to be fixed. When you sit and breathe (in through your nose and out through your mouth) it is best to close your eyes.

Feel the power of your breath.

Your breath keeps you alive. Your breath feeds your body. Your breath moves everything around you. Your breath is your energy. You can breathe out all of the badness you do not want and breathe in the goodness all around you. Once again, this is called meditation. It is a very important part of growing your power.

Breathe OUT the bad

Breathe IN the good

Let yourself feel rested and comfortable. Let your mind rest from worries. Listen for the voice inside you. Feel your belly move, going in and out as you breathe in and out. Breathe deeply. Let your breath go all the way into your heart. Imagine that you are breathing into your heart. With each good breath coming in, you can feel your heart open more and more. Speak to yourself quietly:

May my heart be filled with loving-kindness
May I be strong and happy
May I feel good about myself and others
May all my dreams come true
May I use my goodness to help others
May I use my love to heal
May I only spread loving kindness in the world.

Imagine your heart overflowing with the love and goodness. This love and goodness then spreads through your whole body. It warms you and fills you. You can feel the warmth all over like sweet tickles. Say the words again and again until you feel them in every part of yourself. Feel your heart open up to your words. Remember to keep breathing. Out with the bad, in with the good until you have breathed out ALL the bad and only the good is inside of you. When you breathe correctly your stomach will move out as you inhale and your shoulders will not move at all. This is called belly breathing and it is crucial to all relaxation and self-healing techniques.

Now think about other people you care about. Think about breathing for them and their hearts. Imagine yourself breathing some of the goodness and love you are filled with into the heart and whole body of the person you care about. Send them this warm loving kindness and well wishing. Speak quietly to them:

May your heart be filled with loving-kindness
May you be strong and happy
May you feel good about yourself and others
May all you dreams come true
I send my goodness to help you
I use my love to heal
I only spread loving kindness in the world.

Imagine how you are helping yourself and others. Doesn't it feel good to feel so good and loving? Now sit softly with this good feeling, thinking how wonderful it would be if the whole world were filled with so much love and goodness.

Imagine that you breathe this love and goodness all over the whole world and each and every person, creature, animal, flower, tree, butterfly, ant... every one can feel this wonderful love and goodness coming from you. Did you know you had this wonderful power? Well... you know now and I know you will do wonderful things with it!

Can you feel your own power? Are you filled with warmth and goodness?

Sit tall because you should be proud.

You are so powerful!
You are Goodness!
You are Loving Kindness!

Hold your head high because you are a wonderful person filled with goodness and love who can use your special power to help others. Slowly open your eyes and remember that you are always filled with loving kindness and goodness and strong healing power.

Try to find time each and everyday for this quiet breathing to keep the goodness in you and to help it to grow. Use your breathing power to send goodness and love to other people you know and care about. Every day as you do this, you will grow stronger and your ears and eyes will open wider. You will be able to see who needs love and goodness healing. You will be able to hear the voice inside you, helping you to practice your healing. You will be able to see what other people need to feel better. You will see and feel the light around yourself. You will be able to see and feel it around other people and things. It takes time, but it is worth the wait! His Holiness the Dalai Lama says:

"Take time to develop a good heart
and your life will be filled with happiness."

Time keeps moving and the clock keeps ticking. No one can stop time and the only time you have is the NOW. You must use what you have learned to realize that now Is the best time for this. Now is the time to begin to use your power of thought.

THOUGHTS ARE POWER.

Everything around you was at one time just a thought. If you think you are happy, you will be happy. If you think you are sad, you will be sad. If you think you are hungry, you will be hungry. Whatever you think about soon happens. Thoughts are VERY powerful and you should always try to keep **GOOD THOUGHTS**.

Like your breath, thoughts have much power. If you think you will be able to help someone by sending healing and helpful thoughts—you will help someone. You should always try to think the best thoughts because they keep you happy and healthy too.

These are a few important sayings:

"The same energy that moved thoughts through the mind
moves the stars across the sky."
—*Stephen Levine*

"The happiness of your life depends on the quality of your thoughts."
—*Marcus Aurelius*

"Thoughts are like arrows: once released, they strike their mark.
Guard them well or one day you may be your own victim."
—*Navajo Proverb*

"You become what you think about"
—*Earl Nightingale*

Thinking is like wishing, and the more you think about something, the more important it becomes. You must use your inner voice and breathing meditation to stop thinking of unimportant things and to think only of what is important to you.

Good thoughts bring good things.
Bad thoughts bring bad things.

This is called *KARMA*.

Some people believe that whatever thoughts and energies you send out bounce and come back to you—just the same. Many others believe that these come back one hundred fold. This means that if you think a good healing thought for a friend in need, somewhere, some 100 other people (or angels) are sending good healing thoughts to you. Isn't it wonderful that so many people are sending so much loving goodness to you?

Doesn't it feel good!

But, in the same way that it works for good,
WATCH OUT
because it also works for the bad.

If you send bad and hurtful thoughts to someone... those bad and hurtful thoughts come back to you 100 times stronger. OUCH! You have to be aware of this power and how it works. It is a very strong power—and it works BEST when it is used in a good, loving and helpful way.

Always be aware and careful of your thoughts. Always remember that your thoughts are powerful. Spend time with others who have good thoughts. Stay away from dangerous people who have bad thoughts.

Good thoughts make good things happen.

Spread good thoughts throughout the world!

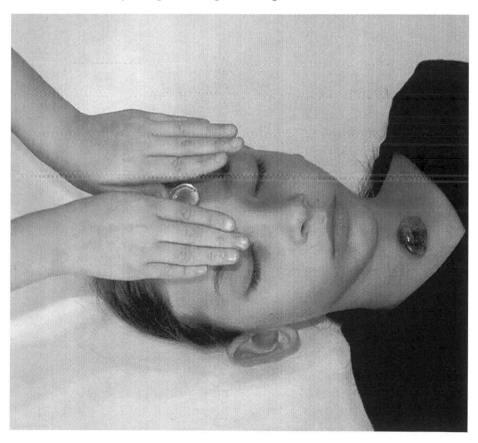

HANDS ARE POWER

You will be using your hands to heal. Your hands will be like magic wands through which healing energy will flow. You must begin to exercise and prepare your hands. Each and every day, look at your hands and think of the power within them.

When you wake up each day, place your hands in a prayer position, this is called the Namaste position. Squeeze them together. Let your palms bend in and out. Spread your fingers open and then close them again. Rub your hands together, imagining that you are washing them clean, all the while thinking of all of the goodness and loving kindness that is inside of you.

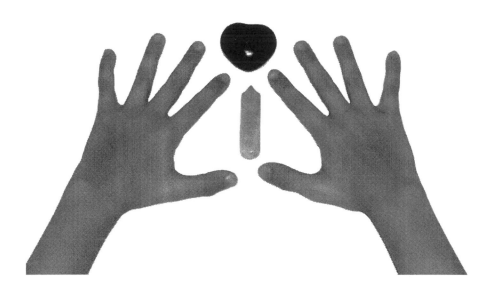

Imagine how you will be using your hands to help people. Imagine using your hands to pull out the aches and pains of your family, friends and of yourself. Place your hands high above your head, still in the prayer position, and then slowly let them come apart and open, slowly, to your sides. Think that you are brushing away all negativity from around you and that you are clearing a space for your self that is clean and pure.

Your hands can be used to push all of the badness away. Your hands can be used to pull pain away. Your hands can be used to send or "beam" goodness, health, and loving kindness to people in front of you, in the other room or even across the world! As you push your hands through the air, you are changing all of the vibrations around you. You are sending your healing vibrations out there, into the world. The more you practice with your power, the more it will grow.

Holding your hands closed or tightened is a sign of tension, and you must learn to relax your hands. When working with Reiki, you will need your hands, as they and the symbols are your tools.

Practice picking up things with your palms. Use your whole hand, and not only your fingers. Hold crystals and stones and see if you are able to feel their vibrations and energy.

Can you feel these vibrations all around you and how you are affecting them? At times you may feel something like a spark or intense heat, do not be afraid, this is normal and as you practice it will soon begin to go away.

You should also do daily Mudras.

A Mudra (This is a Sanskrit word meaning sign or seal) is a gesture or position, usually of the hands, that locks and guides energy flow and reflexes to the brain. By curling, crossing, stretching and touching the fingers and hands, we can "talk" to the body and mind as each area of the hand corresponds to a certain part of the mind or body.

From the little finger to the thumb: each finger represents earth, metal, fire, wood, and water, respectively. So it can be said that the entire universe lies within your ten fingers! It is also said that there is an infinite number of Mudras, even though we only have 10 fingers. Mudras can be used for exercise, meditation or healing.

You may also press or squeeze the sides of your fingers. According to your needs, you can affect both the emotion and the corresponding organ. This is how your fingers work:

- The thumb represents the element of earth; the stomach and worry.
- The index finger represents the element of metal; the lungs, the large intestine and the emotions of depression, sadness and grief.

- The middle finger represents the element of fire; the heart, small intestine, circulatory and respiratory systems, the emotions are impatience and hastiness.
- The ring finger is the element of wood; it is connected to the liver, gall bladder, the nervous system and corresponds to anger.
- The little finger corresponds to water, kidneys and fear.

So if you are ever overwhelmed by an emotion, just squeeze the corresponding finger a few times and you will feel much better!

You may also want to try this: Ask your friend to stand across from you and sound the Oooooommmm sound. Hold your hands in front of you with palms facing your friend. Can you feel the tingle, heat or vibration on your palms?

YOU ARE POWERFUL ENERGY.

In the beginning of time, the people who lived were much closer to the earth and stars. They lived in caves and walked barefoot. They had to hunt or search through nature for their food. They learned to watch the skies for signs of rain or bad weather. They drank from springs in the earth. These people were very close to Nature. Because of this, they were also much closer to understanding and listening to their bodies and their energy.

The world was very still and quiet without tv, electricity and cars and people would sit under the stars in the dark quiet and listen. They had to be keen hunters and the had to listen closely in case a wild animal was wanting to eat them! They lived in a world full of energy and they would hear it, and feel it, and smell it, and see it all around them.

Today it is harder to find this energy because there is so much man-made energy taking up our space. We see the cars, and the televisions, and the bright lights of man-made energy, but we have forgotten to see the light and energy in ourselves and our fellow man.

When we are born we are usually fully open to this energy. We see and feel it all around us. We know of the power it holds and that is why a Mother's smile or simply picking up a baby stops the baby's cries. It is the power of healing touch, where the baby feels the energy connection. As we begin to grow older, we find ourselves in situations that tire us, and take energy out of us. We oftentimes have to do work we don't like in order to survive. We get sick or encounter dangerous and life threatening situations. Growing up we learn to worry, to get angry, to have feel pain. All of this is like a vacuum cleaner, sucking all of our energy right out of us.

The good news is that we CAN get it back!

Of course you may be asking "But where, but how?" "How do I listen when it is so loud all around?" "Where will I be able to find it?"

You will find it in Reiki.

Reiki is the Japanese word for Universal Life Force Energy. When the 'Rei' and 'Ki' are broken down, the Kanji (or Japanese alphabet) definition for Rei is "universal, transcendental spirit, mysterious power, and essence." The word Ki is described as " the vital life force energy." It is pronounced "Ray Key." We all have Reiki energy (Universal Life Force Energy). We were born with it and it is our birthright.

When we begin to learn and use Reiki our level of universal life energy is great and flowing through us properly. We can use this energy to heal ourselves and to also help others with it. A very important difference between Reiki and other forms of energy healing is that with Reiki the healer does not use his or her own energy to heal, so the healer is not tired or worn out after a healing. In fact, the healer is merely channeling energy through him or herself and so he or she is receiving Reiki while doing a healing!

With Reiki YOU too are healed and filled with energy...
all through the process of healing someone.

Although this method of healing has been around since the beginning of time, there was a man who dedicated most of his life to study this method of healing and bring it to the people of today. He lived about one hundred years ago and his name was Dr. Mikao Usui. He was a Japanese man looking for a more meaningful path in his life, and he studied a great deal. He founded a system based on the ways that Jesus, Buddha and other great healers in our history worked with universal energy, simply by the laying on of the hands.

Everyone is born with this power.

Everyone is able to learn and work with Reiki.

You can do it too!

All over the world, Reiki Masters are teaching and giving classes and passing Attunements to re-connect people with this great power, the power that is their birthright. You already have Reiki power within you. You will learn all you need to know about Reiki from this book and after that time it is expected you practice in order to get more experience. The more you practice, the more experience you have. The more experience you have, the greater your connection to this power will become.

Reiki does not require years of study or special schooling. It is passed along from a Master /Teacher to the student through a process called Attunement. An attunement is when you Reiki Master/Teacher channels a very strong current of energy into you with the specific intention that you will be forever connected to the powerful source of the universal life force energy, the Reiki power.

Basically, just about anyone can lay their hands on another person and help accelerate the healing process by transferring magnetic energy and power. What Reiki will do is that you will have a conscious awareness and greater understanding of the power you hold in your hands.

You begin by understanding the basic energy centers in a person's body... If this sounds difficult for you, do not worry because it is not as hard as you may think.

Read the following story out loud to yourself and listen closely to what it says...

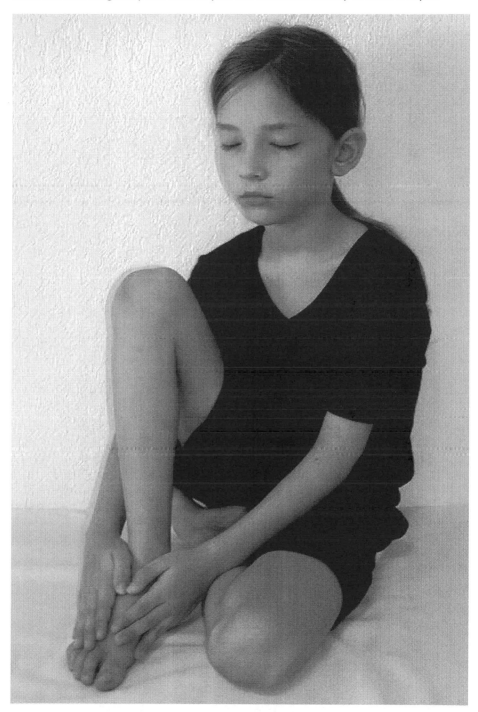

THE RAINBOW TOWER

Once there stood a very tall tower, which reached high up to the heavens. This tower stood firmly on the ground, built out of wonderful solid blocks of light. It was a beautiful tower, more beautiful than any other. This tower was a busy place, where many people lived and worked. This tower had seven stories, and the people who worked on each story were all very different and all had very different jobs and lives.

The people on the first, or bottom floor, were very earthy people, because they lived and worked closest to the earth. They liked to wear the color red and they painted their whole floor red. They sat at red desks, they had red curtains on their windows. They wore red clothes and walked around with red boots. These people were strong and very grounded to the earth. Often times, these people would feel scared or worried. They felt they had to always be on the lookout and were always making plans for "just in case." They often worried the building would somehow break and begin to fall on them.

They walked around the tower, painting red marks here and there where the tower may need repair. They were strong people who wanted to survive anything. They used tools to work with and were always working on something—getting food for the tower, making sure there were enough supplies and that the building was sound. They all wore a big red leather belt which had many pouches attached to it for carrying things. One thing they all always carried was a red stone. They carried this stone out of the way in a pouch which hung from the belt on the center of their backs. This kept it out of the way of their busy work.

Now, the way the tower was built, the sun often shone right into the second floor of the tower. On this floor—the second floor—lived the young people and the people who liked to behave and play with children. There was always some kind of fun going on the second floor. Most times it was some kind of laughter! Others in the tower called them the belly button people because they were always tickling each others belly buttons. They loved the sunshine and playing in it. They loved orange juice and to feel happy and to laugh. They painted everything orange and had orange curtains on their windows. They covered themselves in bright orange wraps, the kind you may use at the beach.

They liked to walk barefoot and some had thrown sand on the floors of their rooms so they could feel the heat from the sun and think they were at the beach. They'd cover themselves quickly in a wrap in the morning and they would play all day. They often wore belly chains, something like a necklace, except for around the belly. Many would also wear an orange stone or pendant on their chain because they liked the color so much and it reminded them of the orange juice which tastes so sweet and which they loved to drink. They had very good ideas and imaginations. They ate lots of sweets and were very sweet people. Everyone in the tower liked to visit with the fun belly button people.

On the third floor from the ground the people were always working on ideas and reading. These were the smartest people in the building because they were very aware of their minds. They liked to gather and discuss science and why things are the way they are. They were very bright people and liked to let everyone know it, and so their whole space was painted a bright yellow. Yellow chairs and carpets, yellow telephones and curtains... they covered themselves in yellow clothing and wore yellow shoes. When you visited with these people, you would feel who you are in the world. They had a large yellow mirror and if you looked into it you would see yourself as you are. Sometimes you may see your anger or your shyness. They liked to help people to see themselves and so many wore a large yellow mirror just over their tummy. When they would pass others in the building, they would invite them to look at themselves in their mirrors. These people could see everyone's feelings. They organized much of the tower because they were excellent decision makers.

On the fourth floor of the tower lived the loving people. When you visited them you would be hugged and kissed and squeezed. These people loved every one and every thing. They also loved the color green because it helped their love to flow. They lived in green rooms with green carpets and green curtains, and they wore green clothes. They cared for green plants and loved to eat green salads! These people felt connected to everything and everyone in the world. They were overflowing with love and were attracted to anything they could put their love into. They liked to wear a large red heart stone over their hearts so everyone in the building would know that they lived on the fourth floor.

On the fifth floor of the tower lived the artists. The whole building could hear them expressing themselves. Often times they would get carried away and people the other people of the tower would hear the shouting "Yes!" of "No!." They had a strong mind and feelings and it was very important for them to do things the way they felt inside was the best way. They were also the best speakers of the tower, and if there was a meeting, it was most often a person from this floor who would do the speaking. Most of the time they would sing, dance and play music. They would color and paint. They would write beautiful music for the whole tower to hear. They loved the color blue and it covered everything they owned.

They had blue walls, blue rugs, blue tiles to walk on. They wore comfortable blue jeans and warm blue sweatshirts. They liked blue jewelry and wore big blue stones around their necks, showing everyone their love for the color and that they lived on the fifth floor.

On the next floor up, the sixth floor lived the people of dreams. Often times the tower was surrounded in a purple haze and the people were so accustomed to the color that soon they took it as their own. They painted everything purple and loved to eat purple popsicles. These people held their head up very high when they walked through the tower. They had the gift of seeing within, which meant that even if you were hiding something behind your back, they would see it. If you were sad but didn't want to talk about it right then, and chose to smile instead, these people would see your sadness.

They all wore purple scarves tied like a crown around their heads and if you needed answers to important questions, you would visit with them. They would let you touch their forehead or eyebrows and suddenly you would get the answers to the questions you have had. They had a very strong connection to inner voices and would often guide you to listen to your own. They knew what was best for the tower and when and if the tower needed any immediate repair.

Finally, on the top floor of the tower lived the Glowing ones. They are always surrounded by beautiful white light. When you visited with them you felt you were sitting on a cloud. Many angels came to visit them. The top floor of the tower was always alight and aglow with warmth, loving kindness and goodness. The light was very strong and blinding and it took all of the others quite some time to be able to look at the people of the top floor of the tower. But when at last they did, they saw how very beautiful and wonderful these people were. They wore brilliant crystal crowns, which were glowing white light. It looked as if a million stars were sparkling all at once. These people had a fountain on the top floor. It was the fountain of universal life energy and they drank from it each and every day.

They created a special waterfall, which allowed this magical water to flow through the whole tower, so that all of the people who lived in this tower could drink from it and feel its loving kindness and goodness power. They made the waters from the fountain flow out into the world and now the universal life energy is in every stream, river, ocean, flower, tree, stone, butterfly, cat, dog, garden... everywhere.

From the inside, and the outside, this looked like a rainbow tower. It would shine and glow with all of the colors of the rainbow. The people within became known as the rainbow people. Everyone who came into the tower could feel the loving kindness and goodness of all of the many wonderful people who lived there. It would make the visitors feel good and warm too.

They would leave to return home and find themselves wishing they could live in the Rainbow tower. Many didn't know where to look. The people on the top floor would whisper to them that they should look within, but many visitors did not hear.

Did you hear?

You have the answer to where you will find it....

LISTEN AND LOOK WITHIN

In your very own body
is this energy and power.

This power lives in you!

Your body is the Rainbow tower.

YOU ARE THE RAINBOW TOWER!

The same way electricity is power, but you cannot see it, you have the universal life force energy flowing through you right now!

Think of the lights in your house. What makes them go on and off? Well, yes... it is electricity—but can you SEE the electricity? No, of course not. Electricity is power but you can not see it. Your body has the very same power. The same way many wires and coils and circuits allow your television and your refrigerator and your lights to work; your body has special places, too.

In your body the electrical system is called...

THE CHAKRA SYSTEM

Chakra is a very old, ancient Sanskrit word, which means wheel, circle or center. It is also often called the "Wheel of Spinning Energy" or the "Round of Becoming." Of course your body doesn't have wires, and coils and circuits, but it does have power. Instead of the electrical power plant, you have the Chakra System. Instead of wires and coils and plugs throughout the whole house, the energy and power centers in your body are called meridians.

These places are the main energy centers of your body. They are the same on everybody, whether they are short or tall, young or old. There are seven main meridians in your body, just like there were seven floors of the tower in the story. Every meridian, or power center, lives in a different place in your body and surrounds that part of your body with specific energy spinning in a clockwise direction. Your major energy places are the same as in the tower where the rainbow people wore their stones. Do you remember?

- The first is the red, at the base of your spine, or lower back
- The second is orange, right around your belly button.
- The third is yellow, above your belly button—your tummy.
- The fourth is green, right in the center of your chest, where your heart lives.
- The fifth is blue, and is located near the place you swallow—on your neck.
- The sixth is purple, it is the center of your forehead at your eyebrows.
- The seventh is the brilliant glowing white light at the top of your head, this area is also known as your crown.

When taken all together your body is like the tower. Your inner voices and guides are like the people who live in the tower. And looked at from afar, you glow, just like the tower, in a rainbow of wonderful light.

Remember, everything in our universe is made up entirely of energy. Light is energy, feelings are energy, thoughts are energy, and even our bodies and the world we live in is energy. When we fully understand that, it will be easier to understand how the healing energy of Reiki works.

Our body is not only the body that we see in the mirror. We are made up of invisible energy that we cannot see. We also have an energy field all around us.

We are beings of energy

and this energy is within and all around us at all times.

To be able to fully allow the flow of Reiki energy through you, you need to be in the best shape you can be in. Did you know that we obtain energy through eating, drinking and breathing? We do. That is why it is important to eat plenty of the right foods! You need to watch your health, eat the right foods, drink lots of water and get plenty of rest. The right foods are raw fruits and vegetables.

Fresh fruit and vegetables are the best foods because they are in their natural state and vibrate at a higher frequency than cooked or processed foods. That is why sometimes people say that raw food is "living food" and cooked food is "dead food." Cooking has taken the energy from the food and destroyed it.

We also need to drink plenty of clean water. Water cleanses and washes away impurities, flushing out the bad and clearing space for the new.
You must also be aware of your surroundings and where you spend much of your time. We are also affected by these "energy fields" all around us. Do you sometimes feel good in a one place and really bad in another? There are energy fields all around us. There are different energy fields just in one room. You can test this by moving your bed in your bedroom. Some places may help you in getting a good night's sleep, and others will make you uncomfortable and likely have nightmares!

Reiki does its healing work on the energy level. Most healing methods work only on the physical level. Reiki is wonderful because it works on the physical, the emotional and the spiritual levels. Our body is a very complex system with many different levels all interacting with each other. (Like the different people, floors and colors of the tower). If a healing treatment is done that only works on one of these levels, the healing cannot be complete. Imagine if the tower repaired only one floor? Or only one row of windows?

True healing must be done at all levels, and that is what Reiki does. It sends the powerful goodness and light energy through the whole person, inside and out.

If you wish to use this power, remember that the energy

will flow through you.

Your body, mind and thoughts must be as pure as they can be.

You must remain balanced within yourself.

The cleaner you are, the better your results will be.

THE AURA

The energy field on or around a person is called an aura. Your breath, your thoughts, your sacred wisdom have all allowed you to drink from the fountain of universal light energy since before you were born. This energy comes into you in many ways—it is flowing all around you at all times and all you need to collect its power is to believe it is there. You need to learn to see and feel it, just like you could see and feel the people in the Rainbow Tower.

You have all of the colors of the rainbow within you.

You were born a very special person, wearing a brilliant crown.

You glow with t his wonderful light and this glow is called your aura.

Everyone and everything has an aura.

An aura is the universal light energy

It is what creates a rainbow glow all around us at all times.

The people of long ago could easily see these colors all around us. That is why in many ancient stories we have been called "The Rainbow People." We are surrounded at all times with these colors. Our aura is the protective energy field that surrounds and goes within our body. Very much like the "halo" that we see at night around the moon, we all have an aura all around us.

Although many of us cannot see it unless we wear special goggles, our inner mind can and does see it on every one and every thing every moment of every day. That is why sometimes a person can affect us in a way we cannot explain. Our inner voice has seen the person's aura.

Have you ever just felt bad when someone came into the room? Maybe this person didn't even speak to you, but you felt bad for some reason. This person was thinking bad thoughts and had bad energy... Your inner voice heard and your inner eye saw the person's aura and warned you to stay away from that person.

To learn to see Auras, practice by sitting in a dimly lit room in the evening. Have a person sit in front of you, in front of white wall. Look closely at the person. Do you see any colors around the person? Focus on their head or face. Try to hold your fingers horizontally, with the tips touching just in front of your eyes. Move them back and forth at different distances until you can see what looks like a little sausage floating in between them. This is when your eyes are slightly out of focus and the best time for you to see an aura.

Try to look beyond the sausage at your friends head or face again. You should be able to see an aura. Try this with different kinds of lighting and background colors. Research tells us that nearly 92% of children can see an aura when they learn to adjust their eyes. You just need to learn to open your "inner eye."

When we do our breathing meditations, we practice listening to this inner voice and opening our inner eye. As we begin to hear it, it helps to show us and tell us about people's auras and what colors they are. The aura is your energy guide.

Always Remember:

Everything has an aura and a Universal Life Energy.

Every human being is a part of the whole.

Your Aura is your energy field.

"All things are tied together. When you cut a tree, whose roots connect with everything, you must ask its forgiveness or a star will fall out of the sky."

—*Lacandon (Mayan Indian) Proverb*

"This we know: the earth does not belong to man, man belongs to the earth. All things are connected like the blood that unites us all. Man did not weave the web of life, he is merely a strand in it. Whatever he does to the web, he does to himself. All things are bound together."

—*Chief Seattle*

When you understand this,

and it becomes a part of all that you know and believe,

you will be ready to learn how to use Reiki.

Are you ready?

THE STORY OF REIKI AND DR. USUI.

Dr. Usui is the originator of the Usui Reiki System of Natural healing

This story has been passed down from one of the students who trained under a Master, which Dr. Usui himself trained, a Mrs. Takata. She tells the story something like this:

One day Dr. Usui was speaking to the students at the university. One day he was discussing the bible and the healings which took place, As he took the podium one Sunday in the late 1800's, Dr. Usui noticed a few curious students in the front row. Odd, he thought because usually students sat at the back. One of the students immediately raised a hand. He told Dr. Usui that all six of them were going to graduate in two months, but that before leaving they wanted to settle an issue. First they wanted to know if Dr. Usui had absolute faith in the Bible as it reads'? "Yes, of course!" answered Dr. Usui. Then they wanted to know if he did believe that Jesus could heal by laving on hands'? Once again, Dr. Usui said that he did believe.

The student said that he and the others also wanted to believe and would Dr. Usui please give them one demonstration. Would he please heal the blind or cure the lame or just simply walk on water, the way the Bible had described. Dr. Usui answered that although he believed these things had been done, he himself had never seen them done nor had he learned to do them. This disappointed the students and deeply troubled Dr. Usui.

Dr. Usui's thought for a moment and then told the students that he could not demonstrate at that time but would someday like to prove it. He promised he would find how to do it and then come back to show them. With that he left the university. He resigned, on the spot and thus began his journey.

The next day he made plans to more carefully study the Bible in a Christian country. He chose America. He entered a university and found that the Bible teachings were not much different from what he had studied in Japan. No one he met there knew how Jesus healed or had seen any healing be done for themselves. No one knew any more than himself.

But, while he was there he also had the opportunity to study other books besides the Bible. He found stories in Buddhism saying that Buddha also healed by laying-on-of-hands. This interested him very much because now there were two great teachers healing people without medicines, only with their hands. So , for the remainder of his time in America, he concentrated on studying Buddhism, hoping to find a formula there for this magical healing power.

When he didn't find the answers in America, he thought that maybe he would learn more if he studied in a Buddhist country. He returned to his own city of Kyoto. Kyoto had the most people and the biggest monasteries in Japan. Monasteries are places for holy men, and he hoped they had the answers or the power. He decided to visit all the monasteries starting with the largest, the Shin monastery.

At the Shin, Dr. Usui asked a monk if the Buddhist Holy books called the Sutras, told stories of Buddha healing. The monk answered "Yes." He asked if the Shin monks had mastered the art of healing the body as described in the holy writings. The monk told him that "We monks do not have time for the physical in reaching the spiritual growth. Spiritual healing is first." This was not the answer Dr. Usui was looking for. Disappointed, Dr. Usui walked away into the jungle to visit other temples. All of the monks' stories were the same. None of the monastery monks seemed to have the power, which could heal.

He traveled on and his last stop was at the Zen temple. Here once again he heard that the monks were very, very busy and had little time for the body healing—but at least they added that they "were sure that someday, during meditation, they would receive that great light and then they would know how to heal." This interested Dr. Usui... Perhaps the answer to his question was in that great light.

Dr. Usui decided to stay on and study all their secrets. He spent the next three years studying the Sutras but without success. He was then allowed to stay on at the Zen temple to study for himself. He loved to study and he learned Chinese, because the Japanese Sutras were translated from Chinese.

He then mastered the ancient Sanskrit writings, because Buddha was a Hindu and he feared that he may have most parts of the story in language translation. While working on his Sanskrit he found a healing formula. There was no mistaking what it was—but the 2,500 year old formula had to be tested.

He told himself. "I cannot guarantee myself whether I will live through it, but if I don't try the test, years of study will be wasted." He was a very determined man and he had promised himself and the students he would find an answer, so he decided it would be worth it to try the formula. He talked about his plan with the head Zen monk. The monk told Dr. Usui that was a courageous man, and that he could perform the testing of the formula at the monastery. But Dr. Usui said he would rather do it on Mount Koriyama, a mountain known as an excellent place for meditation.
Dr. Usui told the monk. "I will follow the formula and test myself for twenty-one days. If I do not come back here on the night of the twenty-first day, then on the twenty-second morning, send out a search party to find my body, for I will surely be dead." Before departing he told the monks, "I shall go through this meditation without food—only water" and on the next day he left for the mountain.

He climbed up the mountain. On the mountain he found an old pine tree near the stream. He gathered and piled up twenty-one rocks that he pulled from the stream and he watered them. He sat with his back to the tree with the rocks before him. He threw one rock away, and then began his first meditation. The monks had taught him how to meditate, and he felt himself opening up. It was now that he expected a something to happen, but he had no idea what it might be or when, and so he sat and waited.

He sat in meditation for a long while. Days and nights came and went. To remember and count the days, Dr. Usui would toss a stone back into the stream at the beginning of each new day. When he grew tired of the meditation, he read his scripture, he chanted, and then he meditated some more. He had no food and all that nourished his body was the water which he had brought to drink. His pile of stones grew smaller and smaller with each passing day and still nothing happened. He liked sitting there and had plenty of time to think and ponder, but the answers he was looking for did not come.

On the twenty-first day, he woke before dawn and sadly, he threw away the last stone. The morning was dark, very black . He could not see the moon or the stars in the sky. Dr. Usui meditated, knowing that this was the last time. He opened his eyes expecting to see nothing, but there, on the horizon, he glimpsed a flicker of light, like a candle!

Immediately he knew in his heart that this was what he had hoped for—and feared. Dr. Usui braced himself. "It is happening and I will be brave—I am not going to even shut my eyes. I shall open them as wide as I can and I shall witness what happens to the light."

The light began to move towards him. It seemed to be coming faster and faster as it got closer to him. Suddenly, Dr. Usui became very frightened, his courage faltered. "Here it comes, the light! I have a moment and a chance to avoid the light, to move out of its way! What shall I do!? If the light strikes me, I might burn!" But then he found his inner strength and he began to brace himself. He told himself " Standing firm is best. I am not going to run away! I'm going to face it! Come, Light ! If this must be then hit me! I am ready!"

With that, he was prepared. He relaxed and, with eyes wide open he saw the light strike in the center of his forehead. The last thing he remembered was himself saying "I made contact." Then he fell backward from the force. When he awoke, he thought that he had died because at first he couldn't see and he could feel nothing. The great light was gone. He heard roosters in the distance and he knew it would soon be dawn.

Dr. Usui sat for a while, very dazed and confused about what had happened. Suddenly, off to his right side, colored bubbles seemed to rise from the earth. Millions and millions of bubbles in rainbow colors danced before him and then moved to his left side. Dr. Usui looked carefully and counted seven colors in all.

"This is wonderful." He thought.

" I was indeed blessed today!"

But that was not all that he saw... After a moment a great white light came at him from his right. Golden symbols appeared; one right after another. They shone out in front of him, like on a movie screen, as if they were saying "Remember! Remember!" He didn't read them so much with his eyes as with his mind. He studied the symbols in front of him carefully and then said, "Yes!" He recalled all he had learned in Sanskrit as the symbols moved in front of him as if they were saying, "This is it, this is it. Remember, remember." After the experience had passed, he said to himself; "I must close my eyes now. For my last meditation please give me a vision."

He closed his eyes and saw the golden symbols in front of him.

And just like that, it was over. "'Now. I can open my eyes." As he regained awareness of his body. He was surprised to find no pain or hunger. "I feel my body is good. I think I am going to stand up." He stood. "My legs and feet are strong. I have had no food for twenty-one days and still I feel I can walk back to Kyoto." For his body felt well fed.

"Well, this is indeed a miracle, for I am not at all hungry, and I feel very light." He dusted himself off, he picked up his cane and his straw hat, and then took the first steps of his twenty-five mile trek back to Kyoto. The Zen monks were expecting him by sundown.

Near the foot of the mountain, Dr. Usui stubbed his big toe on a rock. The blow was hard enough that it lifted his toenail. Blood spurted out and it hurt very much. The pain thumped with his heartbeat. He sat down and held the toe in his hands. Immediately, the pain stopped. The bleeding stopped. "Is it okay?" He wondered?

He continued to hold it a few minutes more until he saw no more reason to hold it as there was no more pain. He removed his hand and looked at his toe, he was amazed and delighted to see that his nail back in its normal position. There was no sign of injury except a bit of dried blood. "This is a second miracle!" He thought.

A short distance later, he came upon a traditional mat and ashtray, which means in Japan that there is an eating place near by and that all are welcome. He approached an old, unshaven man who was starting a fire in a hibachi. "Good morning old man," he said. "Good morning, my dear monk, you are early." The man answered. "Yes, I know. May I please have some leftover rice and some tea, and that piece of Nori you just made? And I would like to have some salted cabbage and also some dried fish, if you have some." (This is a typical Japanese breakfast.)

But the old and gentle man was wise. He had served many monks after their extended meditations on this famous mountain. He knew the appearance of a seven day old beard and by the look of the beard on Dr. Usui, he knew this monk had been without food for a much longer time. "I cannot let you have this rice and hot soup and all those other things, because you are going to have a huge indigestion. I have no medicine and cannot help you. Kyoto is still too far away. You will have to wait until I make a soft gruel for your sensitive stomach."

"Thank you. You are very kind but I think I shall try it." Answered Dr. Usui. He was feeling weak as he moved to a table to wait for the food. The old man thought to himself, "Well, if he wants to do it his way, fine, for I am not responsible." Soon, the man's granddaughter brought a tray with lots of food. She was crying and had a towel wrapped under her chin, tied in rabbit ears on top of her head. "'My dear young girl, why do you cry."

The child sobbed. "Oh, my dear monk, three days and three nights I have a toothache so bad that I cannot stop my tears, and I cannot eat the whole time. The dentist is too far away, so I just suffer and cry." Dr. Usui's heart opened to the child. He stood and put a hand on her swollen cheek. The girl began to blink her eyes. Dr. Usui soon had both hands on her face. She suddenly cried out, "'My dear monk, You have just made magic! The toothache is gone!"

Dr. Usui could hardly believe it. He hadn't really known what to expect from his impulsive action. "Is it really gone'? Are you telling me the truth?" It was true, she quickly removed the rabbit ears and was radiantly happy. Dr. Usui said "Yes, now I believe you are well." The happy child thanked him and then she ran off to her grandfather. "Look grandfather. I took off my rabbit ears!" The grandfather could not believe his eyes. "The toothache is gone? " he said " He is not an ordinary monk, he makes magic!!"

The grandfather walked over to Dr. Usui. "My dear monk, you did us a great service today. We are grateful. We do not have money but for our gratitude. There is no charge for the food. This is all we can offer." Dr. Usui said, "Thank you! I will accept your gratitude. Thank you, very much. Now for my food." With that he turned to his food and eagerly shoveled it in quickly with chopsticks. He ate happily. The people watched and hoped this magic monk wouldn't suffer any kind of indigestion.

Dr. Usui reflected on these miracles, the third and fourth. Placing his hands on the child had again healed almost instantly her toothache in the same way his toe had healed. And he had suffered no ill effects from breaking a twenty-one day fast with a huge meal. 'Now. I am ready for my hike back to the Zen temple. I shall be there by sundown according to schedule." And so he was.

Dr. Usui was met at the temple gate by a young page boy. He asked, "How is our dear monk?" The young boy told him, "Oh, he's suffering from arthritis and back ache. He is in bed near the chapel stove." Before going to visit the monk, Dr. Usui went to his own room to bathe and put on clean clothes. He was then taken to the monk. "My dear monk, I am back.. My meditation was a success." The ailing monk was excited by this news and wanted the details.

Dr. Usui said. "Yes, of course, and while I talk. May I place my hands on your silk covers?" It was late at night when the doctor shared the last happy detail. He was about to leave when the old monk spoke up, "And by the way, my pain is all gone. I can sleep now. I don't need the warmth of the stove, and my body feels wonderful —you say this is called Reiki?"

In English, Reiki means Universal Life Energy.

Dr. Usui slept in a bed for the first time in many weeks. The next morning, after breakfast, he presented a question to all the temple monks. "What shall I do to experiment with this Reiki?" After much discussion, it was decided by all that the best way to experiment was to go into the poorest part of the big city of Kyoto.

This part of the town was home to most every kind of injury and disease including leprosy. Dr. Usui walked there as a monk vegetable peddler—dressed as a monk with two baskets of vegetables hanging from a pole. The beggars assembled quickly. Dr. Usui told them "Please, I would like to be one of you. I would like to live here and I would like you to provide me with food and a cottage by myself. Then you can send me your sick and I will heal them."

The people found that to be a very good trade. "We have all kinds of diseases here, even tuberculosis and leprosy. You are not afraid to touch them'? " The doctor said as a healer he was not afraid of disease and promised he would work sun up to sun down, so he would even want his meals delivered to the cottage.

And so it was agreed. The next day many appeared at his door. Based on his own theory the doctor categorized the sick. He believed disease was an effect resulting from some inner cause. He felt that in the younger patients the cause should be shallow and more easily treated. And this is the way it worked out. The older people required more Reiki treatments and recovery some times took months. The young healed much more quickly. Dr. Usui sent the healed patients to the Zen temple where they received a new name and a job in the city. He told them to become honest citizens, to forget the poor parts of the town and the disease and sickness there.

One evening, after seven long, hard years of Reiki healing, he was out walking through the town when he spied a vaguely familiar face. "Who are you?" He asked. "Oh, you should remember me, I was one of your first healed. The temple monks gave me a new name and found me a job. But now I am back. Begging is easier than working for myself." This terribly saddened Dr. Usui and it was the greatest shock of the his life. He threw himself to the ground and he cried.

More and more of his patients began to return. Dr. Usui soon realized that after all the years of searching for a healing formula, he had been busy with the physical side of life and he had forgotten the spiritual. He had healed the people of their illness and disease, but they also needed healing within.

"Oh, what have I done? I did not save a soul. So the outside body—the physical—is number two and the inner being—the spiritual—is number one. All of the holy writings and the churches were right. I was wrong. No beggars. No more beggars, no more beggars. It is my fault they come back. I did not teach them gratitude. They are here because they are greedy, greedy people. They only want, want, want and offer nothing in return. If I had taught them the spiritual side first and then healed the body, it would have been effective. No more beggars. No more healing."

Dr. Usui felt himself broken. He turned his back on the people and simply walked away.

After a while, the doctor launched a crusade to help unhappy, depressed people. He wanted to brighten their hearts and cleanse their characters, minds, and bodies. He had learned that healing comes by mending the whole person, inside and out. He traveled on foot to every temple in Japan. At each he invited locals to attend his lectures. After one of his lectures, he met a Dr. Chujiro Hayashi, a forty-five year old retired military man. Dr. Hayashi stayed with Dr. Usui until Dr. Usui died, but before his transition, Dr. Usui announced that Dr. Hayashi was to continue this Usui System in the Art of Healing.

Some time later, Dr. Hayashi trained Mrs. Takata. Between 1945 and 1970, she was the only living Reiki Master in the world. Between 1970 and 1980, she herself trained twenty-one Reiki Masters. These masters then went out and trained others in this healing art. Mrs. Takata was about eighty years old when she died. Both Dr. Hayashi and Mrs. Takata practiced and taught Reiki just as it had been passed on by the dear monk, Dr. Mikao Usui.

Reiki is passed on to students through a process called Attunements. I am passing this lesson and powerful method of healing on to you. At the end of this book you will be ready to be Attuned to levels 1 and 2 in Reiki. Because it is passed directly from Masters to Students, it is called a lineage. Your lineage is a something to be very proud of, much like your family tree. It tells the story of where your Reiki teachings came from.

YOUR REIKI LINEAGE

If you decide to pursue your Reiki healing power after you have completely read this book and you decide to receive your Attunements from me, this is what your Reiki lineage will look like:

Dr. Mikao Usui

▼

Dr. Chujiro Hayashi

▼

Mrs. Hawayo Takata

▼

Paul Mitchell

▼

Mrs. Canario

▼

Reverend Reinaldo Torres

▼

Enrique and Mary Cordero

▼

Reverend Fern Alexander

▼

Reverend Dennis Alexander

▼

Reverend Kytka Hilmar-Jezek

▼

YOU

I can and will gladly Attune you. Information on receiving your Attunements through me is available at the back of this book.

Now, before we go any further, please read and spend some time thinking about all you have read so far. It is truly amazing, isn't it?

All of this wonderful power, available to anyone who wants to use it to spread healing and loving kindness throughout the world!

When you return, begin again with thinking deeply about the following quotes:

- **A healing must be performed with good and pure heart.**
- **Each and every person born is a magnificent person.**

- Each and every person born is a spiritual being capable of infinite creativity and fulfillment.
- Each and every person born has the divinity and the power within to achieve greatness.
- It is the birthright of each and every person born, to be made aware of this power and to understand how to use it.

"Seataka is the term in Yaqui meaning PERSONAL MEDICINE, or, One's Personal Power. This power is considered a great gift we are given at birth. The Yaqui believe that we are all born with special gifts and that Seataka is the most important of these gifts. It is to be used throughout life. Seataka is the channel between human beings and the rest of nature."

—*Dictionary of Native American Mytholoy*

How do the above quotes make you feel?

Do you feel responsible and mature enough to tap into this power?

Will you use this power wisely and to
spread goodness and loving kindness?

Do you realize the greatness of the gift you have been given?

If so, then you are ready to begin....

THE REIKI PRINCIPLES

Once you decide you want to use Reiki, you MUST commit to and make a conscious effort to live by the Reiki Principles. These were written down by Dr. Usui, in order to suggest how we should live our lives each and every day. Dr. Usui asked that students of Reiki would hold their hands in traditional prayer position (called Namaste) and think and chant these principles both day and night. He considered these principles to be a great blessing and believed them to be the spiritual medicine for many illnesses. We should remember what is on this list every day, all day long.

JUST FOR TODAY

I will give thanks for all my many blessings

I will not worry

I will not be angry

I will honor my parents, teachers and elders

I will work hard today, and do my work honestly.

I will be kind to my neighbor.

I will have reverence for all living things.

I will be thankful for all I receive

Just for Today

These principles are designed to help you to become the purest channel for Reiki energy. Sometimes it may be hard to follow the principles, but do not be overwhelmed. Try to take things as Dr. Usui suggested, Just for today—one day at a time. It will get easier over time and day by day you will achieve success. Dr. Usui believed them to be a secret way to invite good fortune and a miraculous remedy for many diseases.

Let's look at them and what they mean one by one:

Just for Today

This is easy... Just for today. This is the here and now. Be in the present moment. There really is only the NOW. Yesterday has gone, tomorrow may never even come. Today is all that we have, right now. So work on it in this moment... Today.

I will give thanks for all my many blessings

This simply means to be grateful. You should always feel thankful for what you have as well as what you know will always be provided. You have a home, and food, and warmth, and love don't you? Well then—you need to be thankful for that! We normally live in a state of abundance. Luckily, we have not felt true hunger or true pain. But there are many people in the world right now who do. Be thankful for what you were born with, and what you have.

I will not worry

This is easy too, it means don't waste time filled with worry! Worry usually comes from a feeling of separateness from the goodness and loving kindness—the universal wholeness. Try not to think about or worry about what you cannot control. Do not interfere with timings in life. Whatever is meant to happen will happen, no matter how much you do or do not worry. Do not spend time worrying that things might turnout differently from what we expect. Instead consider only our own advantage and be grateful for your own blessings. Live each and every day to the best of your ability and every thing else will be taken care of.

I will not be angry

Another simple one to follow. Do not get angry. Anger is the result of being out of control. When you feel yourself getting angry, become aware of your reactions. Instead try to feel thankful for having got an opportunity to look at your weakness. Anger is a sign that you are trying to swim against the natural current of events. When feelings of anger come to you, acknowledge them and then let go of them forever.

I will honor my parents, teachers and elders

These people have lived more than you. Life has given them certain experiences which we have not yet encountered. Many of them have seen or felt great pain, great loss, great hunger. As a healer, you must show compassion and respect for these people. They have lived longer and have given a part of their own lives in order to serve. The energies they put out into the universe is a gift and they should be thanked and honored.

I will work hard today, and do my work honestly.

Life is work. Taking proper care of yourself, your things, your surroundings is constant maintenance. Be proud that you have a place to clean, things to put away. Take care of your space, your food, your water... Look at everything in your life as a tool to help you with the healing work you are about to do. In this way, your bathroom sink becomes an altar where you wash your healing hands, your chores become a part of something bigger, of taking care of you, and you are a part of something bigger. Work hard and with love and care. Also, you should not try to cut corners, or sweep the dirt under the rug! This way you are ultimately only cheating yourself in the end anyhow. Being honest with oneself is to face truth in all things. Truth brings clarity. Honesty with yourself will project honesty on to others.

I will be kind to my neighbor.

I will have reverence for all living things.

I will be thankful for all I receive

Always be kind to others. We are all connected. We are all of one source. It does not matter if you do not understand another person... You must not judge or think you know what is in the heart of another person. While they may appear bad to you, their intent may be pure. We live in a world with many different peoples with all sorts of beliefs, upbringing, religions, lives. But they are our fellow man. Be kind. Be compassionate. Be good to them. To show love and respect to all others is to love and respect ourselves and all beings of earth.

Try to remember these principles and let them guide your whole day. Remember that you too are a student of Dr. Usui because you are studying the "Usui Method of Reiki Healing" and you are a descendant of the Usui lineage. Honor the art of Reiki and Dr. Usui by listening to the words that he shared with his students:

Morning and evening

press your palms together

take these words to your heart

recite them with your mouth

REIKI LEVEL I

Reiki Level I will open up the healing channel within you to bring a higher level of conscious awareness after which the Reiki energy can be channeled to heal yourself, other people, food, water, plants and animals.

Just as if you were taking a Reiki class, you are learning about the history of Reiki and the basic hand positions for self-treatment. You have learned Reiki is not a belief system or a religious practice. At the end of this book, the Attunement can be given and you will be able to begin to do self-treatments. This is when you would feel a distinct change between doing your self-treatments before and after the Attunement. Usually you would feel an increase in either heat, tingling or pulsation's, which begin to be felt in your hands.

Reiki Level I also introduces you to learning about and understanding a healing crisis. Many people are full of old "bad" energy and negativity. As you perform Reiki, this bad energy which has been stored or blocked within the body begins to come out, and the first reaction is that people often feel ill. This is normal. It is also possible that the person will experience more pain in the first two or three days of treatment, due to the acceleration of Reiki healing energy flowing through them. Usually, if treatments are given on three consecutive days (as recommended) the pain should dissipate quickly on the third day.

Remember that each person truly heals him or her self. Reiki channels act only as vessels through which you draw the energy you need to create balance on all levels of being. The energy will go to where it is needed the most. The results of the healing may not always be immediately or directly visible. The healing energy may be more needed within the person's psyche and physical ailments may improve only after the inner healing is complete. Never get discouraged. Trust that your healing has helped. Trust that the Universal Life energy flowed through you and went to where it was most needed. Remember that you must allow it to work in the ways it is meant to work. Do not attach your ideas of "power" to it.

You are a channel of healing and loving kindness!

Typically in Reiki Level I class, you would also practice with a partner. You would give each other a one-hour treatment and try to notice any sensations you feel. With a partner, you learn to tell between the differences in heat, which are drawn in different areas of a persons body. Remember that everyone is different. Each person has different needs, and will draw different amount of energy in different areas accordingly. You must practice and listen to the body of the person you are working with. You must learn to give more attention to areas of the body which are drawing more energy.

Practice until you feel comfortable "reading" a persons energy levels. Listen to the sensations you receive and make notes in your mind to remember them. Listen also to what the person tells you. Is the person upset, sad, mad, happy? Over time your hands will be able to feel even more and your will be able to send the proper healing energies to the proper places.

After you become Attuned to Reiki Level I, you will begin to feel different. The Universal Life Force energy will be working within you. It is likely that you will experience a 21 day cleansing period, during which you may feel ill. You may experience vivid and colorful dreams and where things you touch may "shock" or "charge" you. This is all normal.

Additionally, you may dream about the symbols or even symbols, which you do not understand or cannot explain. It is a good idea to keep a journal of your dreams at this time, carefully noting or drawing the things you see. These may very well be YOUR special power symbols.

Reiki Level I teaches you that Reiki is not a religion. Reiki is a very ancient science hidden for thousands of years, until Dr. Usui rediscovered it hidden in the Tibetan Sutras. Researchers at Stanford University, using highly sensitive instruments, which measure the flow of energy forces entering the body, determined that Reiki energy enters the healer through the top of the head (the crown chakra) and exits through the hands. They learned that once the Reiki energy is activated, it seems to flow in a counterclockwise spiral motion.

The amount of healing energy coming from the hands definitely increases during Reiki treatments. There have been people who have videotaped and photographed Reiki treatments with special cameras, which show auras and they actually photographed the healing energy moving through the Reiki practitioners' hands!

REIKI LEVEL II

The Reiki Level II training provides you with the opportunity to Attune to even higher levels of Reiki energy. You will also be Attuned to the symbols, which are used at this level to perform distance healing and a stronger form of mental or emotional healing. Because Reiki Level II activates another level of energy, you will most likely again experience a 21 day cleansing period, similar to the one experienced in connection with Reiki Level I, as your body and different energy centers adjust to an even finer level of vibration.

The Reiki Level I Attunement focuses on elevating the energy of the physical body, so that it may channel more intense healing energy. The Reiki Level II Attunement works more directly on the spiritual body and tends to stimulate growth and development of your intuitive center. It is believed that your intuitive center is located in your pituitary gland. The pituitary gland is said to be the "telepathic" apparatus of the human body. In other words, this is where you would eventually be able to "see" what needs to be helped or healed in the people you are performing Reiki on. People of Hindu origin call this place the "Eye of Shiva." Here, in the West, it is known as the "Third Eye."

Your pituitary gland is infinitely delicate and sensitive, and acts as a sending and receiving station for all mental vibrations. When you are Attuned to Reiki Level II, your "third eye" is opened and becomes more easily focused in both its incoming and outgoing functions. In time, it will become easier for you to receive information on an intuitive level. Your "third eye" will allow you to see your own Higher Self.

By listening and reacting to the voice of your Higher Self, you will find that you are on your proper life path and in a harmonious flow with those around you. Life will begin to take on a pleasant rhythm and all of your activities seem to become synchronized. The higher Self truly knows everything, as time or space does not limit it, and it does not need reason or logic to aid in its activities. Intuition knows because it simultaneously embraces cause and effect, the past, present and future.

Remember: You are a very special part of something bigger...

...something GREAT!

When you learn to open your third eye and you choose to follow intuition, you will find that you will always end up with positive results. You should listen to the voice of your Higher Self. It is always better to listen to the voice of peace and wisdom, which brings your whole being a sense of harmony, than to heed the aggressive clamor of inappropriate desires, which only lead to ultimate dissatisfaction.

Listen to the voice of your heart,

the song of your higher self.

Listen to your Sacred Wisdom!

The more you listen to your intuition, the more it develops. With practice, it becomes easier to follow the guidance of your Higher Self, and increase your confidence, power and wisdom. Reiki Level II gives a powerful boost to the development of this sixth sense, and continued self-treatment using the Reiki symbols help to increase your healing abilities, power and intuition to an even greater level.

You are full of Goodness.

You are full of Loving Kindness.

Healing energy flows through YOU.

You have the power to help and heal others.

Keep your thoughts pure and focused.

You WILL become what you think about.

Keep your thoughts and intentions pure.

As you go along and practice Reiki more regularly, you should be prepared to experience change on several different levels. The changes, which come at different times during your practicing Reiki, result in empowerment. Practice and empowerment then lead to greater responsibility, which is rewarded with greater healing power.

Reiki Level II provides an opportunity to become consciously aware at a higher level. You will essentially " wake up" to further dimensions of your Higher Self. The voice of your intuition will become truly alive, and a greater sense of wholeness, peace and harmony within your entire being will result.

PREPARING FOR YOUR ATTUNEMENT

When you receive your Reiki Attunement, you will forever be connected to the unlimited source of Reiki healing energy and power. Yes, anyone can lay their hands on another person and help accelerate the healing process by transferring energy. But a person who has been through the process of Reiki Attunements will experience a very ancient technology for fine tuning the body, mind and spirit to a much higher vibratory level.

During your Attunement changes will be made by the Attunement energy that will open your entire system, enabling you to channel Reiki. These changes will take place in the chakras and aura and also in your physical body. You may have a strong emotional or physical release as a part of this process. Being properly prepared will help you through this.

In order to improve the results you receive during the Attunements, there is a process of purification which is recommended. This will help the Attunement energies to work more efficiently and create greater benefits for you. Remember that you will be opening yourself up to the greatest power there is. You need to be as pure in mind, spirit and body as you can be. Try to follow as many of the following steps as possible.

Try to eat no meat of fish for three days prior to your Attunement. Try to eat only all raw and living foods for at least three days. Drink plenty of water. Do not use any sweets, and eat NO chocolate or candy. Try to go out into nature and meditate or spend time in complete silence. Give more attention to the subtle impressions and sensations within and around you. Try to get in touch with the meanings. Go for quiet walks, spend time with nature and get moderate exercise. Let go of all anger, fear, jealousy, hate, worry, etc. up to the light.

Consciously create a sacred space within and around you.

The Attunement process creates a healer.

Be ready to accept this honor and power

with the greatest sense of respect.

Your Reiki Attunement is an initiation into a sacred method of healing that has been present on earth for thousands of years. By receiving the Attunement you will become part of a group of people who are using Reiki to heal themselves, each other and the planet. By becoming a part of this group, you will also be receiving help from the Reiki guides and other spiritual being who are also working together to heal the Earth.

It is a wise idea to keep a journal in the time just before and after your Attunement. You should take note of the changes that occur, so that you can refer to them later for a greater sense of personal verification that the Reiki process does indeed facilitate cleansing and healing. It is very important that you actively take responsibility to become more aware and in touch with your feelings.

Every person experiences the Attunement differently. You may feel great changes or you may feel nothing. Most people feel energy flowing in their bodies. This energy shows up as heat, coldness, trembling, quivering, tingling, etc... Some people see colors or images. You may feel a little light headed or dizzy after the Attunement, this is normal—don't worry! To help with this you may want to treat someone or yourself. This will not only help them but it will show you that you have received the miracle of Reiki power! You may have these symptoms for several days. Do not be alarmed, as this is all normal. Your body is simply rearranging the energy and putting it all back into its proper place. You may think of it as the Rainbow Tower getting a Spring Cleaning! The Universal Light Force knows that you want to heal and it is cleaning you out to make you the best possible channel for its powerful energy.

SPIRIT GUIDES AND GUARDIAN ANGELS

Before you get your Attunement, you should do an intense meditation which will prepare you for your Attunements and allow you to meet your Spirit Guide or Guardian Angel. At this time, you will be able to consciously meet and see your Reiki Guide, quite possibly for the very first time! You may immediately recognize your Guide—or sense a very familiar presence.

Your Guide is there to help you as you learn to adjust to the new level of energy and to help you with your healing work. You will learn to hear what your Guides are trying to say with time and patience.

The guidance coming from your Guide can take many forms, including an automatic "knowing" of what to do next, moving the hands automatically, a smell or taste sensation, a sound, or pictures appearing in your mind. Each person interacts a little bit differently with his or her Guide. When you give a healing treatment, your Guide may offer suggestions which come through as automatic knowing of where to go next and of what to do with your hands. You may have specific feelings as well. The more you work with Reiki and use your healing powers, the more familiar with your Guide(s) you will become.

Your Guides will have a definite presence you will soon come to feel and you will be able to recognize and sense the messages they send to you. As you practice Reiki more, you may even begin to sense the presence of others in the area where you are doing your healing work. Very often, other healers or Guides will come to assist you. It is not uncommon for the personal guides or Guardian Angels of the person you are healing to come and assist you as well.

Did you know that every person and even animals have Spirit Guides? They do! It is most likely the working of destiny that the person chose to come to you for their Reiki healing.

It doesn't matter whether or not you choose to believe in the Guides or in Guardian Angels... they ARE there. If you do believe and want their guidance, just ask. Your Guide is there for you... that is why he or she is YOUR Guide!

A final note: never try to listen too closely or look too deeply. Just open yourself up to the feelings and try to "feel" the answers. You never want to use your energy "looking" for your Guide or trying to get an answer. Open your third eye, use your intuition and your Guide will quickly appear.

There are many books available, all of which I have listed and you can learn about at the following sites:

www.ReikiKids.com
and
www.FamilyHealingSeries.com

THE ATTUNEMENTS

Reiki is not taught in the same way other healing techniques are taught. It is transferred to the student by the Reiki Master during an Attunement process. This process opens the crown, heart and palm chakras and creates a special link between the student and the Universal Life Force energies, the ever powerful and infinite Reiki source.

The Reiki attunement is a powerful spiritual experience.

It is a Sacred Honor.

The attunement energies are channeled into the student through the Reiki Master. The process is guided by the Rei or God-consciousness and makes adjustments in the process depending on the needs of each student. The attunement is also attended by Reiki Guides and other spiritual beings that help to implement the process. Many report having mystical experiences involving personal messages, healing, visions, and past life experiences. The attunement can also increase psychic sensitivity. Students often report experiences involving: opening of the third eye, increased intuitive awareness, and other psychic abilities after receiving a Reiki attunement.

Once you have received a Reiki attunement,

you will have Reiki for the remainder of your life.

It does not wear off and you can never lose it.

While one attunement is all you need for each level to be attuned to that level, additional attunements do bring benefits. Experimentation has found that additional attunements of the same level add to the value of that level. These benefits may include refinement of the Reiki energy one is channeling, increased strength of the energy, healing of personal problems, clarity of mind, increased psychic sensitivity, and a raised level of consciousness.

Be prepared and know that the Reiki Attunement often starts a cleansing process that affects the physical body as well as the mind and emotions. Toxins that have been stored in the body may be released along with feelings and thought patterns that are no longer useful. Therefore, a process of purification prior to the attunement is recommended to improve the benefit one receives. You may prepare your mind with intention work and pray in a religious mode comfortable to you to prepare to open to higher spiritual energies and experiences.

Attunements are very precise and can only be transmitted by a Reiki Master who has been trained in Dr. Usui's method. An Attunement is meant to re-open us to the energy of Reiki and connect us once again with that what was ours to begin with, the Power of the Universal Life Energy which is flowing all around us and through us at all times.

Reiki is a wonderful tool to help one develop conscious awareness, the very key to enlightenment. After receiving your Attunement you will be able to do treatments on yourself and on others. Once you are Attuned, you only need to have the intention to do Reiki and the powerful universal life force is immediately drawn through.

You will be able to spread goodness

and loving kindness all around!

Remember to practice regularly on yourself! Self-treatment is the best and most effective technique for total relaxation and stress release. It will raise the life force energy in your body, which will create a balance in both your physical and spiritual body. Treating yourself also helps to release your withheld emotions and energy blocks. It pulls out your fears and worries, your anxiety and tension and it will make a better you!

Always remember and feel strong knowing that once you are Attuned to the Reiki energy, you can never lose it. Even if you don't use it for many years, the moment you do decide to use it, it will be there for you.

You are full of Goodness.

You are full of Loving Kindness.

Healing energy flows through YOU.

You have the power to help and heal others.

Keep your thoughts pure and focused.

You WILL become what you think about.

Keep your thoughts and intentions PURE.

GROUNDING TO THE EARTH

Grounding and centering are probably the most important exercises you will ever learn. Grounding allows you to connect with the Universal Life Force energy and to find your own center. It is at your own center where you connect directly with the spirit and the Universal Life Force energies. Before you begin, make sure you find a place that is quiet where you will not be disturbed.

Sit of stand comfortably with your back nice and straight. Beginning at your toes and working slowly upwards, feel your body relaxing. Slowly feel each part of your body let go and relax. Do this all the way up to your head. Become conscious of your breathing—without trying to control it. Feel the air go in and out as you breathe. As you inhale feel peace and relaxation coming in. As you exhale feel the stress, tension and negativity flowing out and away. Make sure you are breathing correctly. Remember the belly breathing: your stomach will move out as you inhale and your shoulders will not move at all.

As you feel yourself relaxing more, become conscious of roots growing from the base of your spine, growing deep down into the Earth. Roots like tree roots, growing deep down until they touch the energy of the Earth. Feel that energy flowing up through these roots, up through your spine and throughout your body, energizing yet relaxing you. Feel this Earth energy flowing on up through the top of your head, and fountaining up and around you, back down to the Earth again, forming a complete cycle of energy. Feel this energy continuously flowing through you, as you become conscious also of the energy of the Sun and the Sky coming down through the top of your head, flowing down through your spine and throughout your body, energizing yet relaxing you. Feel this energy also forming a complete cycle, and continuously flowing through you.

Now become conscious of where these energies meet and flow together within you. This is your center. For some people, it is at or near the heart, for others it is at the belly button. Breathe into this center; imagine your breath flowing into it and expanding your center. Let your consciousness follow your breath into your center.

Notice what your center looks like and feels like. This is your own very special place. This is the home of your spirit. It is a safe place. None can come here without your express invitation. You make it what it is, or what you wish it to be. Spend some time exploring your center. Anytime you wish, it is easy to return here, just by connecting with the energies and following them to your center. It becomes easier and more natural each time you do it.

Three other meditations you can use for grounding follow:

SACRED OAK MEDITATION

Sit in a comfortable position, your arms resting at your sides. Close your eyes and breathe deeply. Let your breathing be slow and relaxed. See your body as a strong oak tree. Your body is solid like the wide, brown trunk of the tree. Imagine sturdy roots growing from your legs and going down deeply into the earth, anchoring your body. You feel solid and strong, able to handle any stress. When upsetting thoughts or situations occur, visualize your body remaining grounded like the oak tree. Feel the strength and stability in your arms and legs. You feel confident and relaxed, able to handle any situation.

GROUNDING CORD MEDITATION

Sit in a comfortable position with your arms resting comfortably at your sides. Close your eyes and breathe deeply. Let your breathing be slow and relaxed.

Imagine a thick wide cord attaching itself to the base of your spine. This is your grounding cord. It can be a thick piece of rope, a tree trunk, or any other material that feels strong and stable. Make sure your cord is wide and sturdy enough. Then imagine a thick metal hook attaching itself to the end of your cord. Now visualize your grounding cord dropping down two hundred feet below the earth and hooking on to the solid bedrock below the earth. Continue to breathe deeply and notice the sense of peace and stability that your grounding cord can bring you. Replace the cord with a new one each day or whenever you feel your emotions getting out of control.

WHITE LIGHT MEDITATION

Relax, breathe deeply. Take a breath for the count of 3, hold for the count of 3, then exhale for the count of 3. Plant your feet firmly on the ground. Think of your feet growing roots into the ground and getting relaxing energy from the earth. Now think of a brilliant white light over your head. That white light is shining down upon you. Imagine that you are being bathed in that white light. That light is pouring down upon you. That brilliant white light is love and healing. Let that light be within you, and you be within that light. You are getting relaxing energy from the earth and love and healing energy from the brilliant white light.

Now take a minute and see yourself as if on a big screen. You are exactly how you want to be. Picture yourself with everything you want, wherever you want to be, surrounded by people who love you. This is the you that you can become. Look at yourself closely. This is the true you, the real you! Pause and enjoy a moment.
Now when you are ready come back to this place, keep the relaxing, love, and healing energy with you, and slowly open your eyes.

A very good idea is to get a simple tape recorder and to read, very quietly and softly, these meditations onto the tape. Speak clearly and slowly, pausing between each sentence and allowing time for the breathing. When you find a quiet space and time, play the tape quietly and allow your own voice to guide you through the meditations.

There are many good meditation books available for children. I have created a small list of my favorites which you may use to take to the library or bookstore.

Meditation is a wonderful exercise for the brain and relaxing for the body. People who meditate are more focused, calmer and usually more successful!

Try to find these books:

- **Starbright: Meditations for Children**
  Paperback – 112 pages 1st U.S. e edition (October 1991)
  Harper San Francisco; ISBN: 0062503987

- **Earthlight: New Meditations for Children**
  Paperback – 128 pages (August 1997)
  Harper San Francisco; ISBN: 0732258286

- **Moonbeam: A Book of Meditations for Children**
  Paperback – 112 pages (March 1993)
  Harper Collins Juvenile Books; ISBN: 1863711422

- **The Ball of Red String: A Guided Meditation for Children**
  Reading level: Ages 4-8, ISBN: 0829411399

- **Meditation for Children**
  By Deborah Rozman, PhD. ISBN: 0944031250

PRACTICING REIKI ON YOURSELF

The very best way to use Reiki is to give yourself a full treatment every day. You should make the time to start or end your day in this way, gently laying your hands on your own body. Allow the healing energy move into your hands, and then through to the areas of the body which need attention the most. When you begin to practice Reiki on yourself daily, you will find you have more energy. You will feel much less stressed and more able to laugh at the things that would otherwise frustrate you. You will feel more balanced, more calm and happier!

When you take time for yourself to do healthy things,

things you know are good for you,

your body, mind and spirit will respond.

Treat your food with Reiki during the preparation, cooking process, or when you sit down to eat. You simply place your hand over the food and direct the Reiki energy into the food.

You can also treat any medications you are taking and the water you drink!

Remember, Reiki is thought to help increase their power so they work for your highest good and minimize side effects.

It's so easy to do self-treatments! First of all, find yourself a place where you will be undisturbed and comfortable. Make sure that your legs and arms aren't crossed because this is said to block the flow of energy. Start by placing your hands on your head or body with the specific intention of giving yourself Reiki healing energy.

Breathe naturally for a minute or so to relax yourself.

Again, check that you are doing your belly breathing. Your stomach should move out as you inhale and your shoulders should not move at all. Proper breathing is crucial to all relaxation and self-healing techniques. When you can breathe correctly, you will find your energy levels dramatically increasing.

Trust your intuition and let your hands guide you. I used to do self treatments in a specific order, but later came to realize that the hands go where they are most needed. Use the Reiki symbols. Pay careful attention to the sensations in your hands and body and note if they are different with or without the different symbols. You will find that eventually with practice you can give yourself a full treatment without using your hands even once and just focusing on the symbols! (You will be doing a distance treatment to your body from your mind.)

Always begin by making yourself comfortable. You may either sit upright or lie down. Keep your ankles and wrists uncrossed. If you are sitting up make sure your feet are flat on the floor with your spine straight and your shoulders relaxed. Breathe deeply. Calm your breath and thoughts. Rub your palms briskly together to stimulate the blood and energy flow and place your hands in which ever position comes to you intuitively.

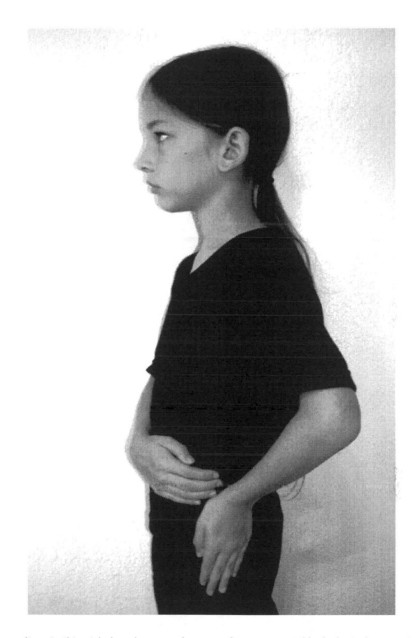

Channeling Reiki with hands over the ears first can quickly help induce a deeply relaxed state. Allow your breathing to be comfortable and natural, breathing into the diaphragm.

You may continue your treatment session by using the traditional and/or optional hand positions, or let your guides show you the way. Be open and experiment and see where the energy takes you. The important thing is that you do it and not that you do it mechanically or in a step-by-step fashion. As your experience increases, you may find that after time you can give yourself a treatment without placing your hands on your body. After time, many practitioners simply flow Reiki into the places they need to.

There is a Reiki saying:

ENERGY FLOWS WHERE THE MIND GOES

Your goal is to strengthen your ability to visualize and use your mind to direct energy.

Allow your self-treatment to continue for as long you feel necessary, but a good guideline is at least 20 minutes. Practice and experiment and find what works best for you. Keep a journal of your feelings.

Give yourself a treatment every day for a week, then two weeks, then a month and re-read your notes in the journal. You will notice your life changing for the better. You will see your powers increase. You will FEEL AMAZING results after that time. It is a habit that is most worthwhile to develop and will only increase your understanding of and capacity for Reiki and healing.

If you plan to use your hands, then start your Reiki session by "washing" your hands (rub your hands against each other about 10 times). This will help energy to flow in your hands. Draw the Cho-Ku-Rei and the Sei-He-Ki symbol over your hands. You may also press or squeeze the sides of your fingers. According to your needs, you can affect both the emotion and the corresponding organ. This is how the fingers work:

- The thumb represents the element of the earth; the stomach and worry.
- The index finger represents the element of metal; the lungs, the large intestine and the emotions depression, sadness and grief.
- The middle finger is the element of fire; the heart, small intestine, circulatory and respiratory systems, the emotions are impatience and hastiness.
- The ring finger is the element of wood and is connected to the liver, gall bladder, nervous system and corresponds to anger.
- The little finger corresponds to water, the kidneys and fear.

So if you are overwhelmed by an emotion, just squeeze the corresponding finger a few times and you will feel better. Try it—it works!

Above all you must practice!!

Practice and perform Reiki on people, on food, on plants,

and most importantly, on YOURSELF!!

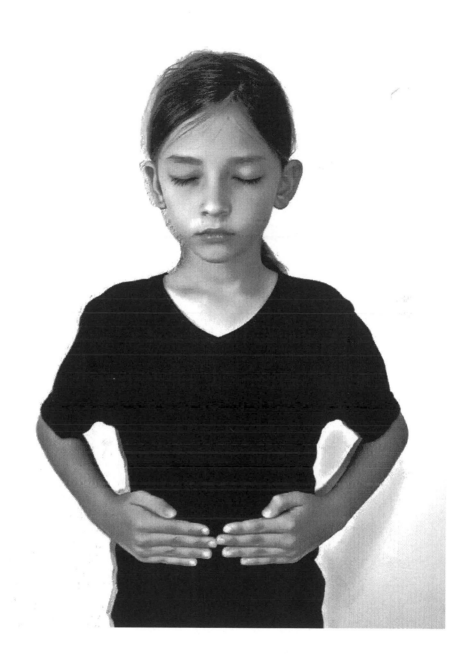

Practice and experiment and find what works best for you.

Keep your thoughts and intentions pure.

Let the power flow through you.

BEFORE PERFORMING REIKI TREATMENTS

I would encourage you to receive a Reiki treatment on yourself. This will tell you all you need about what Reiki can do and you will personally experience how it feels to receive Reiki energy and healing. If at all possible, get a treatment after you yourself have been Attuned, because then you know what to expect and you will feel it even more.

Before you give healing treatments, there are several things you must be aware of and remember.

1. Reiki Healing Treatments are never a substitute for medicine or medical care. Never diagnose any illness, give any specific advice or prescribe anything. You may say what you would do or what someone else you know might have done in a similar situation, but what the person you are helping does do must be their own choice.

2. Prepare the person by telling them that to receive healing energy, no mental preparation or direction is needed to receive a treatment. They only need a desire to receive and accept the energy being sent to them.

3. Never start a treatment when you are angry or upset and never discuss your personal problems. The time of healing is about the other person, not about you. Remember the Reiki Principles and let go of all of your own feelings.

4. Always make sure you are grounded before you begin. Take a moment to pause and do a grounding meditation if necessary.

5. Reiki is often passed without actually touching a person, but rather holding your hands 1 to 2 inches above the person. If you and the person receiving your treatment both feel comfortable, you may actually lay your hands onto the person, but always remember that Reiki means gently touching in a loving and supporting way. Make sure that gentle touch is comfortable for the other person. Remember: Reiki healing energy is available to all of us, at all times. Whether your hands are on or off the person. Your pure intent is the key when it comes to Reiki healing power. My Master always told me "There is no right, there is no wrong, there is only Reiki."

6. Always give Reiki unconditionally and without any expectations. Never promise healing or specify what the energy is for. The Universal Life Force and Reiki Guides will direct the type of energy needed for the healing that is best for the person

you are helping. When you give Reiki, remember that it is not your will that will be done. The Universal Life Energy is only flowing THROUGH you. Sometimes you may hope for a particular result when you work on someone or on yourself and when that expectation is not fulfilled, you become disappointed. This is not right. This is not healthy! Put these feeling aside and learn to wait for the results to manifest. Always remember that Universal Life Energy knows itself what is needed and we must be humble to its power and knowledge by being patient and trusting. Do not fear for Reiki will send the energy where the energy is needed most!

7. Learn the symbols and use them in the correct way. The Reiki symbols must be drawn and used correctly for them to become activated.

8. Keep yourself healthy and alert. Take good care of yourself! Your daily routine as a healer must include plenty of the right foods, lots of clean water, quiet time and meditation, exercise, rest and happiness. Let go of worries and anger by following Dr. Usui's principles. Keep your body free of poisons and foods that will block energy. You never want to over eat and stuff yourself with junk foods or sweets. Eat raw and living foods as much as possible. You must be rested and in good company. If you are surrounding yourself with negative people, their energy will rub off on you. You may need to carefully pick through your friends and decide which ones have been wasting your time and energy and which ones share your common vision and goals for performing goodness in the world.

9. Perform Reiki on yourself every day. Give Reiki to your food and water before you eat and drink. Purify and protect yourself and your space.

10. Call upon Reiki Masters/teachers, Spirit Guides and Guardian Angels before every practice and healing you perform. Remember to ask them for guidance.

11. Keep all conversation positive and caring.

To be a good healer you must

BE STILL.... SMILE... DON'T TALK... LISTEN.

Above all, respect the other person

as you would like to be respected.

PERFORMING A REIKI HEALING TREATMENT

Reiki is never sent by you, rather it is drawn through you. You are merely the channel for powerful Reiki healing energy. Each person draws in just the right amount of life force that he or she needs to release, activate, or transform the energy of the physical and spiritual bodies. When you lay your hands on or over the person you are healing, you should never feel drained in the process. You too are being treated as you pass along or give a healing energy treatment. The energy enters you at your crown chakra and passes through the upper energy centers to your heart and solar plexus. The rest then passes through your arms and hands to the body of the person you are healing.

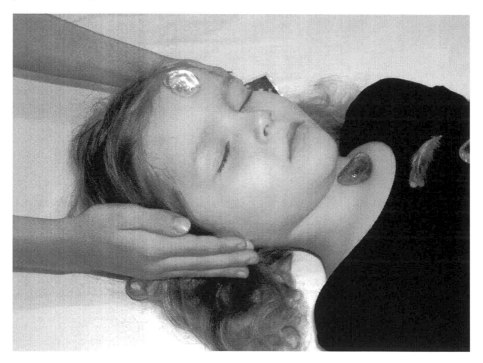

As the Reiki passes through a purified channel in your body, which has been opened by the attunements, the person being healed does not receive any of your negative "stuff." Instead they only receive the pure healing energy from the Universal Life Force. You too are receiving the energy as it passes through you.

As you perform a healing, you will become intimately connected with the person you are working with. At times, you may see visions and images you do not understand. You may experience a brief flash or memory you do not understand. This is most likely what is causing the person pain or blockage. This information may help to guide you in your healing efforts. It may help you to understand the person and his or her problems more deeply.

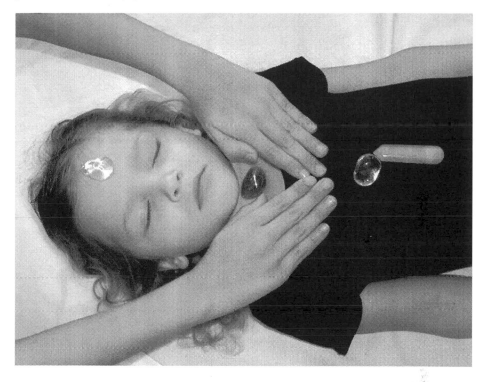

When this happens, pay attention. You may be given insight into how the problems were created and what the person can do to help with the healing. You should share this information only if you are guided to do so, and then only with loving kindness and without judgment.

Always remember that this is sacred work.

Do not share with anyone else what you have seen

or experienced during a Reiki healing.

Additionally, all Reiki healing should begin with a proper scanning.

SCANNING

When you become Attuned, another benefit is that your palm chakras will be opened so the Reiki can flow freely through your hands. Your hands will have an immediate increased sensitivity. You will be able to sense what your body, or the body of the person you are healing needs, and where it is needed the most. The movement of your hands going over a person in search of the area where healing is most needed is called Scanning . When you are scanning, try to hold your breath because the forces are so light that you could easily confuse your breath for a reaction.

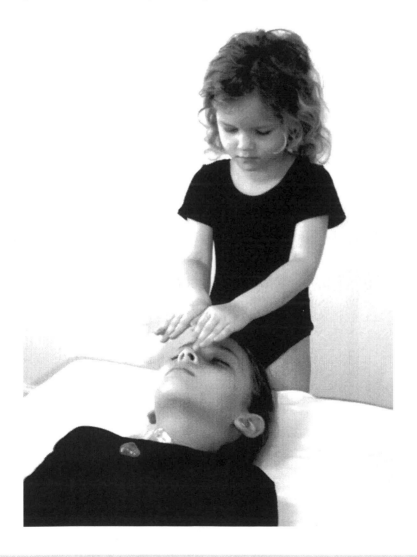

When you perform a scan, first say a prayer asking to be guided to the places where Reiki is most needed. Listen to your guide. Then place your left hand about twelve inches away from the top of the person's head. Think deeply into your hand and sense how it feels. Listen to any messages which may be coming through. Slowly move your hand closer, about three to four inches from the top of the head, and begin moving your hand above the person's face and down toward the feet, continuing to remain about three to four inches away from the body. Make sure your hand is moving very slowly and be aware of any changes in energy that you feel on the palm of your hand.

The first thing you should notice when scanning is the Chakra system. If you are lightly bringing you hand across, without force, you should notice that at certain points the hand naturally moves out, and then, about 3_4 centimeters later, back in, as each chakras is encountered and scanned over.

Now scan again, you may find a spot where your hand tingles, or feels hot, or cold, vibrates, or shakes. Return to the place where the reaction is the strongest. When you feel any change at all, you will know this is a place where the person needs Reiki. Common sensations include feelings of coolness, warmth, tingling, pressure, little electric shocks, pulsations, distortions, irregularity or a pulling sensation. The change may be very slight and you may think it is in your imagination. However, trust your experience. Your sensitivity may not be very developed in the beginning, so you will need to pay very close attention. As you practice, your ability to scan the body will improve.

If you are administering Reiki to someone else DO NOT tell them what you have found, simply use Reiki to heal the irregularity. The reason is that your 'find' may be different from what they are feeling and this will only serve to confuse or frighten the person you are trying to heal. The results of your scan are meant to guide you and to help you send healing to the proper places.

Check the area where you found the strongest reaction at least twice to ensure that no external factors influenced your decision. Move your hand up and down until you find the height at which you feel the most distress. Continue channeling Reiki at the detected spot until you feel the flow of Reiki subsiding or until you feel the area is healed. Then you should recheck, and repeat until no unusual reaction is noticed and until it feels complete. Afterwards, scan until you find another area in need of healing and repeat. You should continue over the entire person until you have scanned and healed the whole energy field all around the person.

Scanning and healing the energy field is very healthy and always beneficial. The cause of most illnesses is in the aura. When you are scanning and treating the aura you are working on the cause and thereby healing problems before they show themselves in the physical body. If there is a definite ailment or problem already developed in the body, the person you are healing will respond better to Reiki if the aura is treated first.

Always perform a scan and heal the aura first. When this is done, you help the person's energy field to accept Reiki more completely and the loving kindness and healing energy will flow in a more powerful way.

Now you are ready to let the healing energy flow, but how and where do you place your hands?

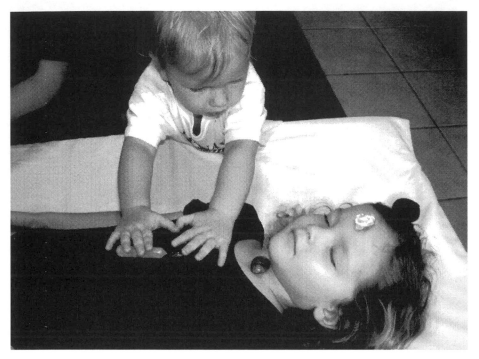

HAND POSITIONS

There are many different known hand positions being used with Reiki today. I am going to share the basics to get your started. Always remember to wash your hands before you begin. You do not need to physically lay your hands onto the person. Do what makes you both comfortable. Remember, everyone is different.

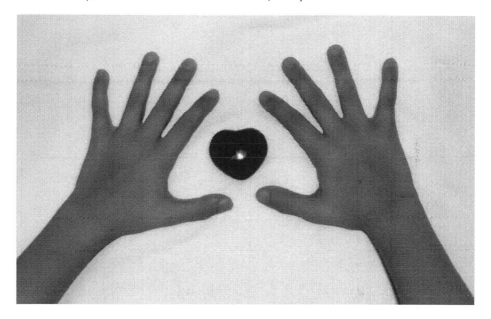

The Reiki energy will pass through

whether or not you actually

touch the person you are healing.

Hold your hands with your fingers together. Make sure you are not crossing you hands in any way and that your arms and legs do not cross. Imagine your hand being inside of a sock... your fingers all touching as if glued together.

COMMON REIKI HAND POSITIONS

1. **Front of the face.** This hand position is used to physically heal the eyes, sinuses, mouth, jaw, pineal and pituitary glands. Emotionally it shuts out the external world, relieves anxiety or stress and promotes relaxation.

2. **Top of head (Placing the heels of the hands above the ears spread out the fingers).** Physically connects the spheres of the brain, helps with headaches, and balances the pituitary and pineal glands.

3. **The base of the skull.** Physically works with the speech/visual centers and the nervous system. Emotionally it eases depression, brings clarity of thought, and helps the body relax.

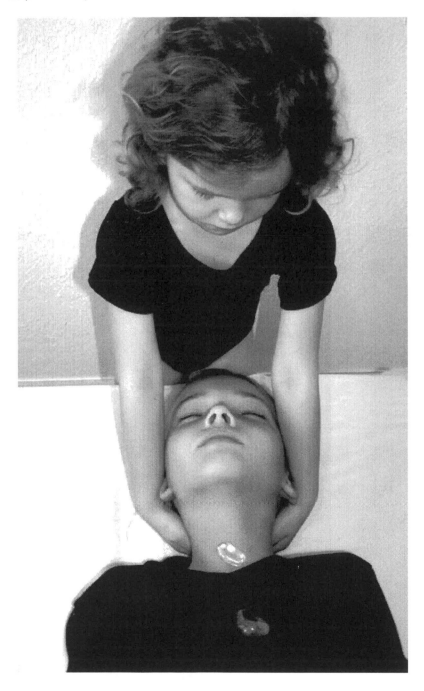

4. **The Throat.** Physically it works with the entire throat region, regulates the blood pressure, and increases oxygen to the brain. Emotionally it helps reduce anger or frustration, increases creativity and self-confidence.

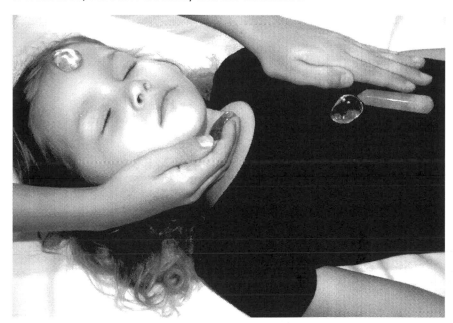

5. **Upper chest (top of the chest with the middle fingers touching).** Physically helps the heart, lungs strengths the immune system and activates the lymphatic system. Emotionally it increases the capacity to love, reduces anger or resentment, and promotes acceptance and trust.

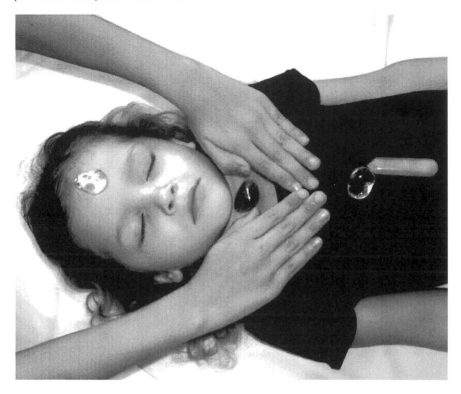

6. **Chest at heart level (just below the breast close to sterum).** Physically it cleanses the liver, spleen, digestive tract, and pancreas. Emotionally it reduces stress and obsessive compulsive behavior.

7. **Mid-Torso (middle fingers touching at navel).** Physically helps with bladder infections, cramps, food disorders and pancreatic problems. Emotionally it helps with hysteria/anxiety and the need to control or manipulate.

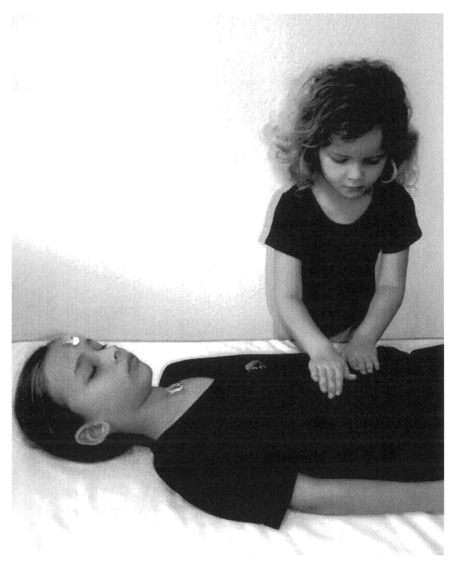

8. **Reproductive organs.** Physically it sends energy to the large/small intestine, bladder, reproductive organs, and urethra. Emotionally it frees you, releases the accumulated fears and opens the creative/intellectual energies.

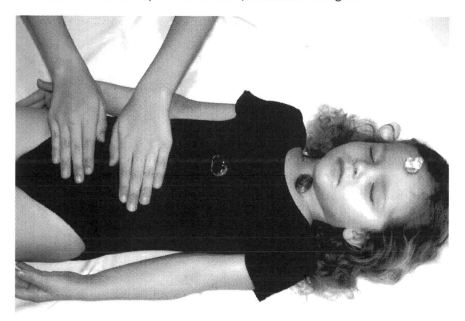

9. **Upper back.** Physically works with the upper spinal column and nerves to arms. Emotionally it releases stored stress and helps with emotional release.

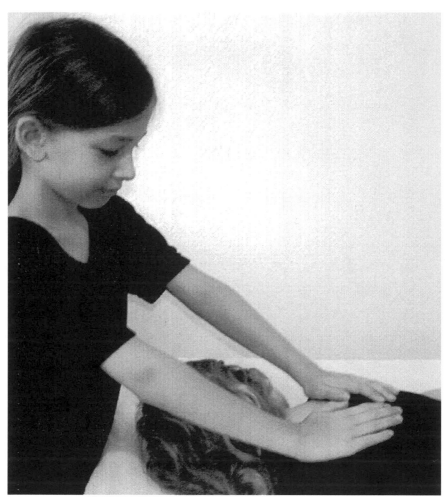

10. **Upper mid-back.** Physically it works with the spine. Emotionally it acts to restore balance to the nervous system.

11. **Mid back (elbow level).** Physically it works with the kidneys and adrenals. Emotionally balances the blood sugar levels and it regulates the adrenal glands.

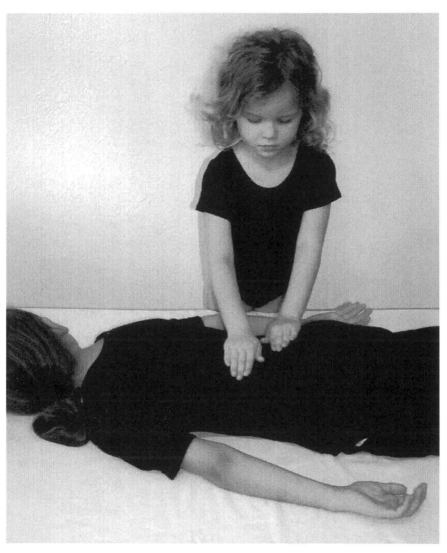

12. **Lower back.** Physically works to strengthen the lower back and grounding. Emotionally it energizes self-confidence.

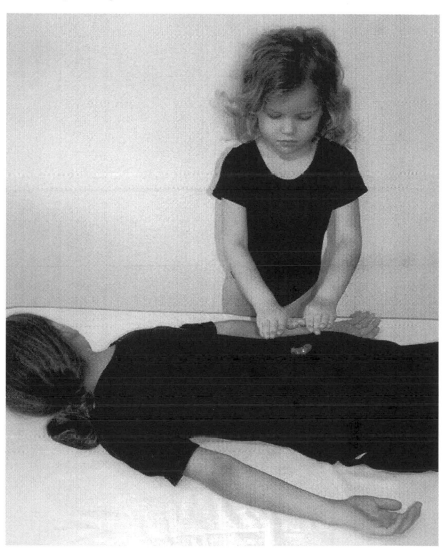

There are many ways to use your hands.

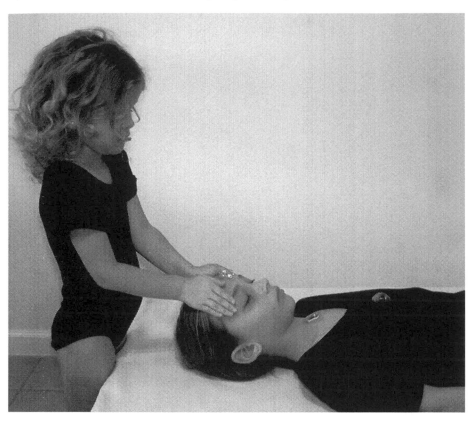

Let the Reiki energy guide you.

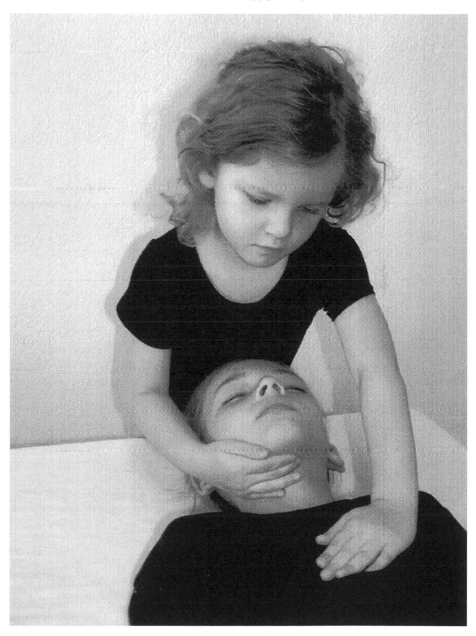

Trust Your Hands.
Trust Your Reiki Power.

USING THE REIKI SYMBOLS

You will be shown three Reiki symbols to work with in this book. Traditionally, you would be Attuned to the first symbol in your Reiki I Attunement and then the other two with your Reiki II Attunement. I believe that you are ready to study all three at once. I believe that you are full of goodness and loving kindness and that you will perform very good deeds and do much good with your power, that is why I am sharing all three symbols with you.

These symbols are very sacred and powerful.

They are the very symbols, which appeared to Dr. Usui in the story you read earlier in this book. These symbols contain the highest vibrations to fully connect you to the universal life energy and bring its power directly to you, to work through you. Please be aware of their power and use them wisely and with the greatest respect!

The powerful flow of Reiki energy will be increased about 15 to 20 times with the help of the 1st Reiki symbol. Your Reiki healing effect will greatly increase in your healing sessions using the first symbol. Using the second Reiki symbol, Reiki will be directed to a more subconscious level. Into the deeper and more hidden feelings and worries. The second symbol will help with inner issues and the person you are helping will be affected positively. The third Reiki symbol is mainly used to send Reiki to any place or person across distance and time.

When you are working with Reiki, you should draw these symbols on to the person or object you are working with. Drawing means that you use your finger or hand movement to draw, over or very near the object of your healing. The symbols should always be envisioned in your mind as being drawn in a violet color.
Every time you draw these symbols, the universal life force energies are activated. You must draw these symbols exactly as they appear so they have the true power. Learn the symbols and when you sit and meditate, envision them.

Reiki symbols do have their own consciousness so it is possible to meditate on them, and receive guidance on how to use them directly from the Reiki symbols themselves. You can discover new uses to these Reiki symbols by simply meditating on them and seeking guidance time. These symbols will be the power in your Reiki healing work.

You may also receive personal energy symbols in your dreams or during meditation. Do not be surprised if you are drawn to symbols outside the Reiki system and not shown here. Trust that they are being shown to you for a reason and use them. Though they are not Reiki symbols, they are for your personal use in self healing and will work for you..

Symbols can also become activated when you use them in a Mantra fashion. This simply means that you chant the symbols' name out loud at least three times, in sets of threes.

All symbols of Reiki are SACRED SYMBOLS

and they must be treated as such.

You should always use these symbols

in a very holy and sacred manner.

CHO-KU-REI

The first symbol you will be Attuned to is the Cho-Ku-Rei. You pronounce this "choke koo ray." This symbol is often called "the light switch" or the Power symbol. Cho-Ku-Rei translates to "Start the energy here." When performing a Reiki healing, this is the symbol which will bless and bring forth the light to you. That is why it is called the light switch... This symbol turns "on" your Reiki healing power.

Art work courtesy of Rev. Dennis Alexander, Sentient Temple

This symbol and its circular shape represent the conch shell symbolizing the calling to the heavens. It is the symbol used to DIRECT and FOCUS all of your power and the effect of Reiki. This symbol is said to call in higher universal energy and accelerates Reiki from low to high vibrations and gives greater focus to the Reiki energy

You may use this symbol on things too, not just people. This symbol can add powerful energy to your food and water, plants and pets, even your personal belongings. The energy from this symbol can clear rooms and crystals This symbol is also used as a protective sign.

Every time you activating the Cho Ku Rei symbol, by drawing it or by chanting it, it immediately clears negative energy and brings balance. By surrounding yourself, your loved ones, and your environment with this divine energy essentially creates a high vibrational field, in which lower vibration/negative energy is repelled or harmonized.

Use the "Cho Ku Rei" by sending it through your minds ever projected into a room where there are agitated people. You can be very creative with its use. When using the Cho-Ku-Rei, you are essentially giving blessings out to your surroundings.

Draw the Cho-Ku-Rei on each palm of your hand before beginning a Reiki healing. Cleanse a room of negative energy drawing the Cho-Ku-Rei on the four walls, ceiling, floor, and in the air, of each room that you go into. You may also use this Reiki symbol in front of any other Reiki symbol that you want to use for any particular purpose. The Cho-Ku-Rei will increase the effectiveness of all other Reiki symbols tenfold.

DRAWING THE CHO-KU-REI

The Cho-Ku-Rei is the easiest symbol to draw. You begin drawing the symbol by moving left to right, top to bottom, and then spiraling into the center in a counter-clockwise motion. The spiraling motion must break the vertical plane at least three times.

Remember , it spirals counter clockwise. We are connecting with the creative whole of Universal Life Force Energy when we do this. In the Eastern spiritual tradition, this represents moving our consciousness out from the earthly field and reuniting with the unconditional love, wholeness, harmlessness, and oneness where all creation emanates.

SEI-HE-KI

The second Reiki symbol you will be Attuned to is the Sei-He-Ki. You pronounce this "say hay key." This symbol is used primarily for the feelings and emotions of a person. Sei He Ki Key," translates as "Man/Woman and God Becoming One." It is called the Protector Symbol and is connected to our deepest thoughts and feelings. Doctors and Scientists agree that all sickness begins with one's feelings. This symbol can help to heal those feelings.

Art work courtesy of Rev. Dennis Alexander, Sentient Temple

This symbol may be used treating and correcting bad habits. The Sei-He-Ki works on the subconscious level—meaning that you don't even have to think about it. It goes into your mind and takes finds where these feelings and worries have been hiding. This symbol also helps to balance the right and left sides of the brain. Use it to help you find misplaced items. Use it to help you memorize or remember things.

DRAWING THE SEI-HE-KI

The symbol is drawn in nine distinct movements. This symbol works on negative energy and is used for mental and emotional healing.

HON-SHA-ZE-SHO-NEN

The third Reiki symbol is called the inter-plane connector, distance symbol or the absentee healing symbol. This is the symbol, which will allow you to send Reiki, across the room or across the world—through time and space. You can send healing energy to a persons past or send Reiki into the future. This is a very powerful symbol.

You pronounce it as Hawn Shaw Zay Show Nen. Its translation means "The God in me reaches out to the God in you to promote enlightenment and peace." Using the Hon-Sha-Ze-Sho-Nen symbol will allow you to beam Reiki to people sitting at a distant place. To do this you should do all three Reiki symbols, hold your hands with palms facing outwards and visualize the person between your two hands and start beaming Reiki healing energy!

Art work courtesy of Rev. Dennis Alexander, Sentient Temple

This symbol will also empower your goals. Write your name and your goal on a piece of paper and draw all three Reiki symbols on it. Give Reiki on the paper for 30 minutes each day. Remember to continue active work to achieve your goal. Soon you will find you have achieved your goal!

DRAWING THE
HON-SHA-ZE-SHO-NEN

This symbol is also called the Twenty-Two symbol because of the twenty two distinct movements in drawing this symbol. There is new information out from Japan on this symbol. It is believed that these distinct twenty two patterns can be divided into four parts and that they have several meanings. These four parts are 1) the Five senses, 2) the Five elements: Earth, Air, Fire, Water, and Spirit 3) the Tree of life and 4) the Swirl of life .

LIFE AS A HEALER

What a wonderful gift you have, to want to help others. You are already on a wonderful path just be having an interest in doing good.
Remember:

Thoughts are power

and if you are thinking you want to do good,

good will be done!

The first thing is to always live by the Reiki Principles. Whether or not you chose to become a Certified Reiki Practitioner, you will help yourself greatly by living this way. The principles are simple and easy ways of living in harmony with the universal life force energy. People who live in peace tend to live happier and more productive lives.

To help keep yourself in the flow, it is beneficial to do a nightly self-evaluation. Review your day mentally and think back to how you reacted to each person and situation.

What was appropriate and what could have been changed?

What do you remember most clearly?

This exercise will help you to become aware of your behavior. With practice, you will begin to see yourself watching yourself. Ask yourself "what old habits need to be broken"? There must be a willingness to review one's actions each day, and see what could have been done better. Also with practice, you will begin to see yourself catch yourself before giving an old inappropriate response in a new situation.

You will find that some patterns of behavior, such as good manners are quite positive. What we can add to these positive patterns, to make them even more effective, is our conscious awareness. In other words, when you say "Hi" to the passerby on the street, don't just mumble it out of habit. Look the person in the eye and feel yourself connect. You will feel so much more alive, and this will help the other person to feel the same way. When you walk down a crowded street, consciously send love out to those around you—it will make a difference.

Be nice to your family members and siblings as well. Do you know that very young children can feel and use the Reiki powers too?

They can!

Share what you have learned with your younger siblings.

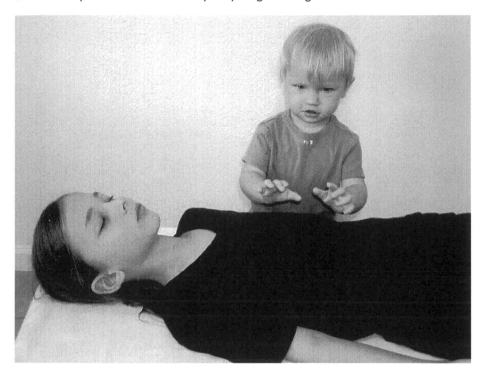

The wave of gratitude will flow through you, and with practice staying consciously aware, will begin to take less effort.

It is always good to give yourself a Reiki treatment at the end of each day as well.

You also have to be very careful and aware of what you take into your body. The author of this book, and the children photographed in this book are all on a raw, sometimes called "Living Foods" diet.

What does this mean?

We all only eat food that is not cooked.

"How can that be?" you may ask. It does sound a bit strange when you first think about it – but it's really not. Our family chooses to eat this way because it makes us feel healthier and stronger.

Most people think that to be healthy and strong you need lots of meat and potatoes, but nothing is farther from the truth. Look at the mighty gorilla. He is one of the strongest animals on the planet and what does he eat?

Leaves, fruits and seeds.

Our teeth are made for chewing and our digestive tract is made to pass food through it very quickly. Foods such as meat clogs our digestive tract and sits inside of us much too long. This makes our bodies have to work harder and longer just to get this food waste out.

A happy and healthy body is one which takes in lots of greens and fruits, vegetables, nuts and seeds. These foods give us the strength and the power we need. These foods allow our bodies to spend time working on things like building strong cells, muscles and bones instead of always working on digestion.

Raw Food = Raw Power

THE RAW OR LIVING FOODS DIET

Many people believe that cooked food is dead food. We all know that when something goes into the fire, it is usually destroyed. In very much the same way, the living enzymes and vitamins in your food are destroyed when your food is put to the fire (cooked).

Did you know that as human beings, our bodies have evolved over a four million year period? For 3,950,000 of those years we humans ate only raw, living foods! So if you look at it in this timeline, it is only very recently that we came up with the idea of eating cooked food.

Our greatest fuel = water!

Did you also know that we humans are made up of between 60 and 70% water! We are. The first thing that happens when we cook food is that all of the water content is lost. Fresh vegetables and fruits are loaded with water, and therefore made perfectly to replenish us and keep us "working" at our best. Cooking food also destroys about 50% of the proteins in our food and denatures the remaining 50% of proteins in our food. This also makes them much harder to digest and for our bodies to utilize.

Did you know that fresh fruits and vegetables are a powerhouse of vitamins and minerals? But when the very same fruits and vegetables are cooked, between 50 and 80 percent of the vitamins and minerals are also destroyed.

Remember to breathe!

We also need air to survive. We need fresh oxygen to be able to function properly and to think clearly. That is why we discussed the proper breathing and meditation techniques earlier in this book. Cooking makes the oxygen of the foods lost and free radicals become produced. Free radicals are just as bad as they sound; little monsters inside causing all sorts of disease and chaos in our bodies!

Most importantly, enzymes are destroyed whenever our food is heated above 118 degrees. That is much lower than the average cooking temperature of any cooked food.

Enzymes are very important to our functioning. They are the catalysts of every chemical reaction in our bodies. Without enzymes there can be no cellular division, immune system functioning, energy production or brain activity. Vitamins and hormones cannot do their work without enzymes.

Our bodies contain two different types of enzymes in our bodies; metabolic enzymes and digestive enzymes. The human body stays very busy and can produce over 100,000 different enzymes, each doing a unique task.

The wonderful clue to our eating only living and raw foods is that every living or raw food contains exactly the perfect mix of digestive enzymes to break it down completely. These are called food enzymes. Food enzymes perfectly break down the food within our bodies, allowing us to take exactly what we need and quickly discarding the rest. Mother Nature sees that all raw and living food decomposes and returns to the earth from which it came.

But heat destroys enzymes so cooking our food leaves us with a large mass of food going through our system that isn't breaking down properly.

The enzymes necessary to digest our food have been destroyed. This causes many problems. It begins with our body not being able to metabolize the cooked food. Suddenly partially digested fats, proteins and starches are stuck inside of us and eventually they will clog up our body's intestinal tract and arteries.

The human body is a miracle and it recognizes this, so it foes to work immediately to "borrow" enzymes from our reserves to try to get the cooked food out. But each and every cooked food meal we eat will cause this enzyme production. Soon our reserves will become very drained. This is why so many people are having disease and need help these days. They are eating three very rich cooked meals a day and the body is running out of ways to cope with this unnatural strain.

There was a man named Dr. Paul Kouchakoff, who in 1930 found that when we eat cooked food, our bodies attack it with leukocytes, the white blood cells that are the cornerstone of our immune system. These cells bring enzymes to the cooked food in an attempt to break it down and get rid of it.

This simply means that our bodies actually treat cooked food as a foreign invader! The body wants the cooked food OUT! The body needs living and raw foods coming in.

This also explains why you are so tired after a large meal, like at Thanksgiving. Did you ever wonder why everyone stuffs themselves and then just lays on the sofa or slowly climbs the stairs to take a nap? It is a tremendous burden on your body to produce digestive enzymes and leukocytes.
Did you also know that we actually burn close to half of the calories we consume in a cooked meal just to digest it! That is a lot of wasted calories and energy, wouldn't you agree? All of that energy would be saved had we fed our body what it needed rather than what we were used to eating out of habit.

We also tend to overeat.

The people of long ago didn't eat the way we do today.

Not even the Kings had a full breakfast, lunch and dinner as we do nowadays. People planned their food consumption carefully and far in advance. They stored food and canned it to save for a later time. They didn't have drive-thru's and refrigerators. They were lucky if they had a large meal once a week.

People of the olden days were also wiser about fermenting foods and had an instinct to create sour krauts and sprouted breads and cakes because these products aid in your enzyme function. Look at all of the animals in nature and how they maximize their enzyme reserve.

If you give a squirrel a raw nut, it will not eat it, but always will bury it. It will only dig it up when the nut has sprouted. The squirrels have found sensors in their noses that can identify a sprouted nut. Raw, un-sprouted nuts have enzyme inhibitors that prevent the nuts' food enzymes from digesting it. Only when it sprouts are these inhibitors deactivated. That is when the squirrel will return for and eat the nut.

When our bodies are eating the wonderful raw and living foods they were meant to be eating, we are in optimal health. All of our cells, organs and systems are able to do the jobs they are capable of in perfect balance. A healthy body requires proper enzyme capacity, acid-base balance and a healthy digestive tract. These are all achieved through a raw or living foods diet.

Raw and living foods give us a life free of pain and disease.

Raw and living foods lead to a longer, more energetic life.

All of the energy saved from digesting cooked food is put towards much better use. The main focus of your body becomes one of cleansing and rebuilding. You will find that you even need less sleep. Your thinking becomes clear and you will feel calmer and much more rested!

Your body will be satisfied and working at its top level of performance if you treat it correctly and feed it what it needs. Your body will repay you for this kindness by producing the correct balance of hormones and brain neurotransmitters. You will be more alert, more aware, more in tune with the Universal Life Energy. You will be pure.

Changing to a raw and living foods diet can be fun too. It's fun to eat yummy puddings and cakes made from fresh fruits and sprouted grains. It's an adventure to look for wild foods in nature and to "bake" our food in the sun. How many other kids do you know who are allowed delicious smoothies and dried fruit cookies and sweet carob bars at all hours of the day?

A raw and living foods diet makes you a clear and pure channel for your

new Reiki healing power and energy.

The purer you are the better and more

powerful channel you will become.

Try raw and living foods for two weeks (without cheating!) and see how wonderful you feel and how much more in tune with yourself and your universe you become!

RAW AWARENESS

When you eat a completely raw diet, you become much more aware. When you go out in nature, animals begin to show themselves to you because you no longer smell like a dangerous "hunter" human, but a fellow gentle creature. The fact is, you begin to smell different. A human body is self-cleaning, just like that of an animal. When you are raw you don't need lotions and perfumes, deodorants and mouthwashes. All of those smells come from the digestive process and the cooked food which is rotting inside of your system, waiting for more of those reserve enzymes to push it out.

When you are raw, your senses fully awaken.

You can see more clearly, hear more precisely, and smell everything! You sense of taste becomes alive and the freshness of fruits and vegetables, nuts and seeds become overwhelmingly delicious. If they are not too tasty to you now, it is because you are used to the cooked taste... but as your body cleanses itself, your taste sensations will change and in no time you will see how very wonderful a fresh fruit picked off the tree can become!

Because you have all of this extra energy and your senses are awakened, you become so much more aware. The creatures and beings in nature also become much more aware of you.

My children, the children photographed in this book have had wild foxes, deer and squirrels come up to them in nature and eat from their hands. They have found wild birds with broken wings who have allowed them to touch them and carry them to safety. They often speak of their Spirit Guides and the news their Guides share with them.

Raw food brings you closer to nature and the universal way. For more information, I have included a list of books you may want to read.

- The Raw Life by Paul Nison
- Feel-Good Food A Guide To Intuitive Eating by Susie Miller and Karen Knowler
- Nature's Path To Supreme Health by David Freedom and Tierra True
- Raw Kids by Cheryl Stoycoff
- Spiritual Nutrition And The Rainbow Diet by Dr Gabriel Cousens MD
- Living Foods For Optimum Health by Brian Clement
- Survival In The 21st Century' by Viktoras Kulvinskas
- Nature The Healer by John and Vera Richter
- 12 Steps to Raw Foods: How to End Your Addiction to Cooked Food by Victoria Boutenko

- Something Better, God's Original Design, Live Foods by Katy Chamberlin
- Raw Family by The Boutenko Family
- Intuitive Eating by Humbart Santillo
- Food Enzymes: The Missing Link To Radiant Health by Humbart Santillo
- Conscious Eating by Dr Gabriel Cousens MD
- Blatant Raw-Foodist Propaganda by Joe Alexander
- The Sunfood Diet Success System by David Wolfe
- Nature's First Law: The Raw-Food Diet by Stephen Arlin, RC Dini, and David Wolfe

I have included this list because eating a Raw and Living Foods diet has changed our lives. As a Reiki Master, my awareness and feeling of power multiplied a hundredfold! It was amazing that after 30 days on an all raw diet how in touch I became with the Universal Life Force energy.

Our family has not been sick and we all have so much more energy. I have had contacts with nature and Spirit Guides which I am sure I would not have had, had I continued to be burdened with the time and energy draining digestive process.

It is a big change and a big step, but I feel one, which is necessary if you want to be the purest channel for Reiki healing power and energy.

Your body is your temple—you should treat it as such!

RAW COOKBOOKS

Getting started on Raw foods is oftentimes difficult because people tend to think that raw and living foods means only eating the fruits and vegetables off the trees, and after a life of cookies and cakes, that does sound kind of bland. But there is so much more to raw foods than that!

I have compiled a list of our favorite raw food un-cook books, which offer hundreds of wonderful and tasty recipes for cakes, breads, burgers... We eat very well and always feel satisfied after a meal. My children like that they are in charge of their own health and love to come up with and create recipes of their own.

I hope you will use this list as a guide to some of the best books available. Sadly, many of these titles are not at every library.

Do something about that! Take this list to your local library and make a request for these books if they are not available.

Or you may ask your parents to order them through the link at our web-site at www.ReikiKids.com.

- The Sunfood Cuisine by Fred Patenaude
- Vibrant Living by James Levin, MD and Natalie Cederquist
- Angel Foods by Cherie Soria
- Hooked On Raw by Rhio
- Raw: The Uncook Book by Juliano
- Uncooking With Jameth & Kim by Jameth Dina and Kim Sproul
- Warming Up To Living Foods by Elysa Markowitz
- The Raw Truth: The Art of Loving Foods by Jeremy Saffron and Renee Underkoffler
- The Raw Gourmet by Nomi Shannon
- Not Milk...Nut Milks by Candia Lea Cole
- Living With Green Power by Elysa Markowitz
- Living In The Raw by Rose Lee Calabro
- Garden Of Eden Raw Fruit & Vegetable Recipes by Phyllis Avery

THE HEALING ALTAR

It is a good idea to keep your spiritual healing things in their own special place. The energy they contain is powerful and sacred. Most people create an "altar" where they keep these things. An altar does not have to be very fancy or elaborate. It can be on top of your dresser, on a night stand or a book shelf. A good thing about inside altars is that you have a permanent place for your things and you see it often.

Some people like to keep one outside. Outside alters work best if you have a special box which holds your things and you can easily carry them inside in case of bad weather. A good thing about an outside altar is that you are in touch with the natural elements all around you.

Take your time setting up your altar. Make sure you have chosen a place where you will be able to focus and conduct spiritual activity. It is nice to visit your altar each day. You should use your altar as a focal point to connect you with your goodness and loving kindness.

When you decide where you will place your altar, ask an adult to assist you in the proper preparation and ceremony. You will need the following:

- 1 white candle
- 1 small smudge stick (these are available at metaphysical stores)
- 1 cloth (on which to place your items)

When you have found the right place for you and are ready, light your white candle and smudge the area. You should ask that the area be cleansed of any bad energy and that the area always be filled with goodness and loving kindness. You should perform a simple blessing ceremony for the items you place on your altar. A simple blessing ceremony follows:

This is my altar, may it always be surrounded by love.

I ask for Blessings on my altar.

May I gather strength at my altar.

May I gather goodness at my altar.

May I gather loving kindness at my altar.

Dear Altar, protect my sacred things.

Bless them with power to help me when I help others.

Bless them to work their power of goodness through me.

Allow the flow of love around my altar

to keep my things safe from harm.

Next you should choose what you will keep on your altar. You should keep things which give you inspiration, strength, power, happiness, feelings of love. Some ideas for your altar are: a medicine bag, crystals or special stones, sea shells, feathers, nuts or seeds, bowls or goblets, incense, statues or drawings of sacred beings, the Reiki symbols, holy or spiritual books, pictures of your loved ones or sacred places, diary, journal, coins, chimes, bells, essential oils, holy water, runes, candles, musical small drums, divination tools, anything else you feel gives you special power.

WORKING WITH CRYSTALS

In recent years, using crystals in Reiki healing has become very popular. Crystals help to amplify and direct Reiki energies. You may begin by holding your crystal between your hands and charging it with Reiki power. When you use your crystals in a healing, you will be able to feel the amplified energies.

Choose your crystals carefully and make sure they will work well with your energy field. The color, size and shape also matter, so always choose one that feels best to you. Allow your mind's eye or your Spirit Guide to guide you in making a choice.

After you have chosen and purchased your crystal, it is a good idea to clean it with some salt water and then keep it in the sunlight for three days. Also, try to expose your crystal to the moon. Then charge it with Reiki using your 1st and 2nd Level Reiki symbols.

Use your crystals for your own self-healing or for those you wish to heal. Hold your crystal over the body and guide Reiki energy to the body. Visualize Universal Love and allow the Reiki energy to flow through it.

Remember to recharge your crystals regularly. Draw the symbols onto them when you do this.

YOUR ATTUNEMENT AND REIKI CERTIFICATE

So... You are now at the end of the book. Congratulations for having such an interest in how you can better yourself and the world around you.

Do you feel ready to be Attuned

to the wonderful powers of Reiki?

I can Attune you distantly and provide you with your Reiki Levels I & II Certificate via our web site at:

www.ReikiKids.com

When you feel you are ready, just contact me through the link at the web site and we will arrange a time and date that I will attune you. Or, you may write me a letter and a calendar date that is special to you, and I will plan to Attune you.

Please send your letters to:

Family Healing Series
Attn: Reiki Attunement
6822 – 22nd Avenue N., suite 345
Saint Petersburg, FL 33710-3918

Remember it may take up to two weeks to get your mail, so please schedule at least 1 month ahead.

The entire Attunement process will take about 20 minutes. We do not need to meet, and you do not need to travel far. You may sit down and enjoy it in the comfort of your own home!

Once completed, you will be a Certified Reiki Practitioner.

I will mail you a lovely professional Certificate and copy of your Reiki lineage. You can contact me with questions before or after your Attunement. Additionally, after you have been practicing Reiki for some time and you feel ready to teach Reiki or to perform Reiki healing on a more professional level, I am also available to Attune you to the Master/Teacher level.

For Master Level I will need you to write me a letter describing three experiences you have had, and also 1 letter of recommendation from someone on whom you have performed Reiki.

At this time Certificates are free, but we do work with several charitable organizations, so your donations are appreciated.

GUEST CONTRIBUTION
BY SUZIN CARR

HE KNOWS THE SPIRIT IS WITHIN HIM

I watch my 9 year old son, Chandler, playing with his puppy in the yard. Most often he is patient trying to teach him how to sit and stay, but his favorite lesson is "the ritual." It is a calming lesson after wild play where they sit together and let go of all their extra energy until they are almost completely still. When it is over, Chandler tells Buster that he is released and free to go. There is suddenly an amazing calm in both their Spirits. Why is that?

I like to believe that Chandler came to us from the Galapagos. He was a gift as it were for our tenth wedding anniversary, conceived out of great love and hope. I felt connected with his Spirit long before I was even pregnant, so I was not the least bit surprised to find out that we would be having a baby. Excited, yes, to say the least. In the beginning, the doctors firmly believed Chandler would arrive on July 2, but my heart knew it would be June 23. After many months of family bets and discussion, the week of June 23rd arrived. The prenatal visit confirmed that July 2 was still the date and I should just go about life in anticipation of what was to come. On the morning of June 23rd, my husband was full of empathy for me knowing how much I truly believed this child should be arriving. He feared for my disappointment, but instead to his surprise he found out it was indeed time to welcome this baby. At 8:02 that evening, we held this special child; this blessing that I have always known has a clear and definite purpose and who is meant to be here. June 23 is a day for Chandler, "our bringer of light."

In the year before Chandler was born, I came to find answers to questions I never thought to ask. Answers that worked for me about holistic health and healing, organic foods, and a less is more philosophy. I began to realize that there are really no coincidences in life if we look deeper at the details of how a situation or thought unravels. I believe that, now more than ever. I studied different literature, devoured articles on making better life choices in one way or another, and began to meditate in a way that worked for me. The day Chandler was born, I felt very little discomfort up until the very end and was able to fully witness the miracle that happens when life enters one world from another.

As most new parents can understand, I could not look at him enough. Everything about him was and is so completely perfect. He was made in the image and likeness of the God that we believe in; that is so evident in the Spirit we have witnessed throughout his life. I remember vividly watching his life through the sides of his eyes and imagining all the wonder that his mind was holding. Enough so, that one day very early in his life I wrote a poem entitled "Vision" to question what God looked like to Chandler. I know he saw His face in the clouds; I prayed my mind would not be so cluttered to miss it.

Life has taken us on a journey of ups and downs as it does for most folks. The "ups" times show us a child literally shaking with the excitement at the thought of a gift. The "ups" times also show us the same sleeping baby we once had, just now a bit older. The "downs" of scrapes and falls have led us elsewhere and to share some of what I studied in the years prior to his birth until now. Chandler knows that his angel is Uriel and that his Angel mantra is "I am never without the light of God." Nothing beats Chandler's heartfelt rendition of "This Little Light of Mine" by voice or guitar. When he falls or is tense, he knows to use his Light fingers to draw away that energy and create a new place and space for healing. Remember, please, there are no coincidences. I have seen him on more than one occasion comfort a crying friend and minister to them with words like "send it away" or "it is not a part of you." I have used healing touch with him from as far back as I can remember; teaching him to take healing breaths and how to visualize a different outcome. Together we have pictured fevers breaking, calling on the glands to release the sweat and allow the temperature to drop. I have witnesses to this effect on many occasions, and they are in awe of that mind/body connection. He knows to picture himself well and whole and complete. We are connected without a spoken word, but always when we are still and quiet.

Our morning ritual has always included a prayer for the day in the order of "Thank you God for this day. Please keep us safe and well; happy and loving you. Seeing Your face in all we do; hearing Your voice on our heart. We ask you to guide us, protect us and keep us safe always. Amen." Our Faith has called us to be grateful and aware of our blessings throughout the day, giving a Grace at a meal, seizing the moment to help, regardless of convenience. The night time begins with prayers and then a thank you to our bodies. Saying goodnight to them and giving them permission to rest, refresh and rebuild. We take in deep healing breaths to fill our lungs and every cell in our bodies. Mindful of how hard each part has worked on our behalf; honoring every cell. We send the "extra" stuff out with our light fingers from our heads down through our feet and back to Mother Earth. It is time to rest. Our day's ritual is over.

One night not too long ago, Chandler had difficulty falling asleep. I went in to remind him that "you are perfect, and strong and filled with God's Peace and the power of the Holy Spirit" only to have him call out most indignantly "I know THAT!" My heart was full that night and peaceful at the same time. I know he "gets it."

His interpretation and understanding of God from our kitchen table church tells him that "Faith is being sure of what we hope for and certain of what we do not see. Hebrews 11:1" He knows in his heart and readily believes that everything he says or does will either have a positive or negative effect on the Universe. He knows that every choice he makes, he chooses. He gets it that he is part of a much bigger world than he can ever know. He knows that we are all connected, and that we are constantly breathing in and out atoms and cells from other living things. He knows that when he focuses, his mind can have the most amazing effect on his body and Spirit. He is wise beyond his years, and often beyond his parents as well.

While Chandler has always been a most inquisitive, trusting and open soul, I believe that most, if not all, children are capable of similar experiences if given the tools. Studies show how receptive young children are to learning skills and foreign language because their minds know no limitations. Their Spirits are free. They have a language all their own and are generally not "put off" by something different. To support that, I am certain that there was never a child who thought Chandler's light fingers or healing words were odd. I believe most found comfort in them. I know that he does.

This year has brought us to a new place where Chandler has illustrated a book that I have written. The drawings are all his own, and they are priceless. Wanting to know a child's perspective of how it happens, recently I asked him for his thoughts about choices and on healing. "God is everywhere, Mom" he said. That is enough for me.

So often I find that I am bound by my own limitations of what I think I know or what I expect to experience. When I breathe in and distance myself emotionally, and sometimes physically, from a situation, I frequently get a clearer view. Each of us has the ability to do that, but we find ourselves wrapped up in the details, no matter how irrelevant they are. We forget that we are choosing to be right where we are, and if we don't like it, we can always choose again. There is no magical formula; there is just the Spirit, and that is enough if we allow ourselves to see it clearly.

Chandler knows that the Spirit is within him. He lives it, breathes it and honors it every day of his life. In teaching him, he is teaching me. I have learned so much from watching an uncluttered soul draw in energy to change his Universe. It, too, is a miracle in itself. There is no journey; there is no end. There is Life and it is happening at this very moment, if we will only be still and quiet to let it reveal itself to us.

—*Suzin Carr*

Suzin Carr has been married for 20 years, is the mother of Chandler (the illustrator of "I Choose" for children and "I Choose Too!" for grown-ups), is the former Guv'na of Lutz, and is in constant awe of the Universe and how connected living beings are to one another.

Please visit her at www.illuminatedpublishing.com.

Peace is possible...one human at a time.

Choose well.

GUEST CONTRIBUTION
BY HEIDI CANALES

REIKI FOR KIDS: MY HANDS ARE TINGLING AS I WRITE...

"Why would kids need Reiki?," I mused as my Reiki teacher spoke so lovingly about her work with children. Being one of those super loving and saintly, patient people, I just assumed that she loved to do Reiki with children because she is so loving to all people. She had given me my first Reiki session, which was soul cleansing, cathartic and accelerated my being's vibration to a level that I had not before even comprehended. Yet, there I was, transmuting into a Lighter, more sensitive spiritual state in that session. But, was this right for kids?? I thought of my 7 year old daughter, precocious in many ways and wise beyond her years, then stored away the idea that perhaps she might one day have some interest in this weird, wonderful Reiki scene I was immersed in.

The truth is, that I was so deep into Reiki for my *self* at the time, I was far from being ready to share it with anyone else. My training and attunements took a good amount of time and dedication. The amount of time and growth needed to integrate Reiki into my being and life took about a year, and that was just the beginning!

The other truth is that, when I first had Reiki session then studied it, I had just recently left a job as the Director of a Prisoner Re-entry Program. With a B.S. in Experimental Psychology and a Master's Degree in Counseling, I brought years of counseling, social work, knowledge and wisdom into the prisoner reentry program. Never having been imprisoned myself, I somehow had a knack for working with criminals, young and old. My staff and volunteers worked on an impossibly low budget to provide the necessities people leaving incarceration required in order to not return again. The work itself was incredibly rich in depth and immediacy.

Transitions are one of my specialties and I was given many opportunities to help the toughest and neediest in our county get back on their feet and stay on the right track. However, day after day, there was never enough money to help everyone; there were few resources. There were millions of reasons to give up.

Yet, it was in that tiny, run down modular office and in the jail visiting rooms that I learned about that very tenuous, nameless thing that transcends barriers, that breathes past pain, that hopes beyond the seemingly impossible blockades in life. Jail and prison lighting is strange, eerily grey and life draining. Year, decades of living in a cell can and does shred the desire to live, destroys any notions that trust is possible. And listening, listening, asking the hard questions, then hearing the harder answers revealed something shocking and unexpected, always unexpected , even to a seasoned veteran like me.

I saw the "broken child" in these faces and it was there that their raw spirit would reveal itself as Light, as sacred, and as very lost.

Broken children with criminal histories—the most dangerous people in my county. Not all were willing to open up and bare their souls, and after knowing what they had endured at the hands of their abusers, I wasn't inclined to push. My way was to create an environment of trust, respect and hope. To capture my client's willingness and to reflect back the strength and power in their vulnerability. With the door closed, even in the jail visiting rooms, through metal bars and Plexiglas, the "broken child" would sometimes come forward and I found this to be the ultimate opportunity to teach compassion, to help my client connect the dots between their victim pain and helplessness as a child and their crimes, addictions, violations of self and others in their adult lives.

The soul energy of the suffering inner child was profoundly, intensely real and when we shared the knowing of its presence, there was a bond created between us and with the Light. So many of my clients were at odds with any concept of God or Higher Power, so "Light" became a way to honor that sacred, pure core that is always present, can never be corrupted or lost.

Time was always an issue-my time as a Director was not supposed to be spent mentoring clients, yet the word got out that "Heidi can help you-talk to her; listen to her." I so deeply wanted them to connect with their own Light and to stay in that place we created together-one of honor, forgiveness, even holiness.
Before long, I knew that my real 'job' was to raise money for the program and to maintain powerful political alliances. There was not enough time for me to counsel and visit in the jails and prisons. However, the greatest 'success' stories always involved a staff member or volunteer who made that visceral, human/spirit connection; the roots and branches of that relationship were birthed and fed through one vital ingredient: Hope.

I held hundreds of these "broken children" in my heart, my auric field, my prayer. In this way, Reiki was birthing me through this job, with these people who were held in utter contempt and deemed hopeless by much of society. Reiki's Light flashed deeply and shook my very DNA the first time I experienced it and I instantly knew that all I had learned and done before was leading me to my Souls' authentic path-to be a vessel for healing. Having witnessed some of the most devastated lives turn gently to the Light ,to walk one more day, to try one more time, to fathom that the Light is Love and is eternally for each one of us-this witnessing, this communion and transition into meaningful life, was what I was destined to do.

During a Reiki III class, my beloved Reiki teacher was talking about working with children and teens, even infants. Her own woman-child aura was so divinely beautiful and powerful that I felt it was time to practice Reiki on my 7 year old daughter. I gave her the full treatment: on my massage table, silk eye pillow, hand placements, blessings, even sage smudging before and after. With ethereal Reiki music playing in the background, I entered this sacred space with my daughter. She was quick to hop up on the table and what happened next was a gift I will never forget. As I prayed over her, blessed her and worked with her energetically, the full meaning of 'trust' emerged. As our Angels, Guides and Holy Ones joined us, I was gifted with knowing the essence of "intention." My hands heated up quickly- her small, lovely being received each ray of Light as she spoke so naturally of her angels and her energy moving, with colors and images that reflected how very close to the Divine she was/is.

And I was humbled, barely holding back tears, so full of gratitude that, in spite of my many mistakes as a mother and as a very flawed human being, my child was open with a spirit that sparkled, flew and accepted the highest and purest of energies.

Reiki with Children, whether "broken" and middle-aged or teens or minutes old... I believe, is an honor, is truly healing, grace-filled, and enriching.

I silently vowed to be Reiki, live Reiki, flow Reiki, share Reiki, always connecting with the child. My hands are tingling as I write this and my heart chakra feels so peaceful...

These moments of bliss, merging with the Divine and entering Light drenched spaces in time are often fully realized when challenged by their energetic opposites...yin and yang ...enter the Oppositional Teenager!!!

Dear reader, I apologize for the sudden shift in Reiki focus, yet I must tell you the whole truth. I honestly portrayed my evolution into Reiki through professional experiences and tried to convey the core intimacy of Reiki with my daughter, yet I would be amiss if I left out the some of the road bumps that jolted me into reality and shaped my fuller learning about Reiki with kids.

Not all kids are 'into' Reiki! Can you imagine how unprepared I was to hear my 15-year old son tell me that I was crazy, that Reiki was totally weird and he didn't want me doing it to him, ever? My son, who had been chronically ill, very isolated and depressed...my son, whom I love and wanted to share this Light and healing with, was blocking me from the very start. He refused Distance Healing. I could all but hear the non-Light entities snickering with glee as he scathed me with his judgments and stormed off, again and again. Oh, but couldn't I run to my husband of 20 years for support? He also thought it was weird and a waste of my time and education. Surely, my best friend would salve my charred heart and cheer me on to my Soul's work?

Yes, she actually did defend my intentions, but would not let me give her a Reiki session-she is just not a 'touchy-feely person'. All was not lost. After all, I am a person who can motivate, inspire and work with resistance on a level that most would run from. My son could sneer at me and proclaim me utterly insane, but he could not intimidate his beautiful Guardian Angel. I learned that even with the highest degree of skepticism and resistance, I could appeal to the Angelic Realm and keep trusting, trusting!

You'll never believe who is starting to connect with the Light and even seeing Reiki as a viable healing tool—yes, the ultimate cynic, my son, and his equally skeptical dad. Go figure. The same young man told me just the other day that a friend of his saw his aura. I asked my son if he wanted me to tell him what color it was. He did and the look on his face was priceless. I got it right. Perhaps I am now only half nuts. It's all about hope, remember?

Not too long ago, I was asked to give Reiki to a colleague's teen children after doing a Reiki energy clearing of their office space. The son was 15, and a true Indigo child; the Reiki energy flew through him; he felt the balancing in his chakras and manifested many good results from his mini session. He even wrote me a professional recommendation! His sister, 13, was less inspired, but felt very calm after the session. Their young cousin, who had recently lost his father to suicide, accepted the Reiki and healing in his soul, allowing my being to merge with and strengthen his with Light.

Such an honor that words fail me.

Because I am also a lifelong psychic, I naturally tune into my clients using these gifts, for which I don't yet have words. Always grounding my work in the Light, I clear non Light away, flow Reiki, bless, protect and do whatever the Holy Ones guide me to do. Since trust is so essential in this exchange, I always explain what I'm going to do and make sure everything is comfortable each step of the way. Children are especially receptive to visualization; their imaginations are less encumbered.

When Reiki and Light begin to fill and manifest in yourself, your family, your home, even your mundane tasks, the synergistic effect is awesome!

As a Reiki Master and a wife, mother, friend, etc., I have seen the positive effects of Reiki, whether on an adult's 'broken child' or a child of any age! In spite of some obstacles along the way, I have loved learning from others and assisting their healing with this ancient energy art, melding the physicality of human touch with energy of the highest source. Thank you for honoring me by reading this labor of love! I am ever grateful to all the children who have blessed me with their trust and their deep soul work. I know that all of creation benefits from their growth and courage!

PS—My daughter considers herself a Reiki Practitioner! We wish you all Reiki Blessings!

Deep Peace,

—*Heidi Canales*

Reiki Master: Tibetan, Usui, Chikara
Psychic

You may contact Heidi Canales directly at: hkc001@gmail.com

CONTRIBUTING THOUGHTS

"I have just completed "Reiki For Children" and found it to be a very comprehensive, complete study for children. Having spent my time teaching Reiki to Masters, of other studies, I found myself extremely impressed with the ability of the children trained through this introductory book. I personally trained a young man who studied this manual and at ten he is now a Reiki Master. Dr. Jezek has done an outstanding job."

Dr. Dennis Alexander Usui Master/Mayan Shaman/Karuna Reiki Master/Teacher

"I really enjoyed this book. It is an amazing resource of information for both Reiki as well as the importance of eating raw foods. I would recommend this product to anyone who'd wish to teach Reiki to small children."

—Marcela Decuir

"I know Kytka from the Waldorf Homeschoolers Site. I knew very little of Reiki and raw foods before purchasing this ebook. What led me to purchase this particular book was the gentle and effective way Kytka expresses herself with the written word. This makes it all the much easier for a newbie like myself to take on new ways of thinking and doing things. Another thing that drew me to this book was the photographs she chose to use. Just seeing her children actually doing what she was writing about makes you want to learn how your children too can use their energy for good rather than evil. Kytka offers a beginner a gentle read into the background of Reiki with tips on how you and your children can integrate this form of healing in your lives. She is also a Reiki Master which enables her to atune you (qualify you) during the different stages of attunement. I enjoyed this book and have shared it with my husband who was also a bit interested in this form of healing. As an added plus, you do not have to spend $1,000's of dollars on your attunement-- Kytka offers it all to you at a very reasonable cost and nearly free of charge. All purchases with Kytka I have had have always been dealt with in a professional manner."

—Misty Mama

"This book is the most comprehensive children's book on Reiki I have ever read. It is wonderfully illustrated, and masterfully written. Any child will benefit from this accurately composed work. Too often today, children are not given the opportunity to study that which will bring them peace in a stressful world. This book is most timely."

—Dr. Alexander

"Kytka Jezek is a gentle, sensitive and feminine guide through the initial steps for the practice of Reiki. This book is a wonderful intro for children (and adults) to the world of Reiki. The entire book is truly a well thought out volume. My 12 year young son and I so enjoyed her whimsical explanation of the chakras and the meditations are, yes, absolutely a magical transport."

—Marie Ondine

"Any child who studies this book will benefit enormously!"

—*Dr. Timothy Scott*

"As a Fourth Level Reiki Master I was skeptical about teaching a four year old Reiki. However after reading "Reiki For Children" and seeing the children who trained from this book in action, my skepticism disappeared and I honor these wonderful children for a job well done. I have no doubt that any child who studies this book will benefit enormously.

—*Dr. Fern Alexander Usui Master/Teacher Mayan Shaman/ Karuna Reiki Master Teacher*

This is a subject very near and dear to me, I had my youngest daughter in my 40's after my master attunement. She seemed very distressed after the birth and as an infant, it took me 3 months to figure out that she needed an attunement. (this was 15 years ago so there was not really much of a support community) I did her 1st at 2 months and her 2nd at 3 months... (she is now 15 and wanting me to do her master, yes I am holding off till she is a bit older)

I started teaching her as a toddler about the fireflies in her hands that would take the "owies" to the grandmother. The hardest thing I had teaching her was that she could not keep the owies. I had to develop a whole new vocabulary for reiki and energy work since she was so little. As the mother of 6, the biggest thing that I noticed about her behavior was the calm she had as a toddler. I never seemed to have to teach her compassion and such it was just there. We have had some close calls with the shrinks at school understanding her frame of unconditional love and state of no fear, which o them was abnormal.

She became a Lakota fire-keeper at 7 , and now at 15 I am still amazed at her state of no fear which I really believe was a result of her Reiki attunements.

—*Debra Townsend*

My nephew is a very sweet boy, early connect with spiritual subjects. Once, when he was 7 year old, he was feeling a strong headache and I've asked to his mother (my sister) if I could apply Reiki. With her agreement, I' did that, asking him if he'd like my help. It was a very simple and nice moment, because he stayed very quiet and he got totally well in a few minutes. Since this day, sometimes he asks me to do "that magic thing with the hands."

His reaction was very spontaneous and I've transmitted him some Reiki principles in a simple language. He asked me to learn Reiki, but my sister think he is still very young to understand. I don't think so, but I've to respect her decision. I've told to my nephew I will back to this subject in the early future... So, we will have a very nice boy practicing Reiki from the heart.

—*Sandra Maria de Sousa Pereira*

FINAL THOUGHTS
BY BRIAN VASZILY

HOW TO BE HAPPY AND SUCCESSFUL:
A LETTER TO MY SON ON HIS GRADUATION

IMPORTANT NOTE: On June 7, 2009 my son graduated from high school. I wrote an abbreviated form of this letter below on the inside flap of a book I gave him … one of a small handful of the works of art that truly helped me center my life years ago, and several times since, called The Tao of Pooh.

Discover more about The Tao of Pooh. The world should read this little classic, especially now.

Meanwhile, this letter below is for him as he prepares to enter college and his adult life, but I present it to all of you in the belief that you may find some strong value in it too.

And in the hope you will pass it on to others who you think may benefit.

After all, we're all in this together.

> Dear Evihn,
>
> As an adult, only I have changed my life. Because as an adult, only I can finally choose to do so. Or not.
>
> Even if things happen to me that are beyond my control … a bird pooping on my head, an earthquake tearing my home apart beneath my feet … only I can choose how I will respond to it.
>
> But other things help me, and have helped me, in my choosing to change. These are beautiful things … these are the catalysts and guides. And whether it lasts for decades or moments, I call the interaction with these catalysts and guides "intense experiences."
>
> Nature has often provided me these intense experiences. Go to her often, including when nothing else seems to provide you the answers you seek. She may provide you answers, often by instead reminding you of the real questions, if you allow her to.
>
> And it is also often other people who have provided me these intense experiences.

The Always People

This certainly includes the people who love me; even though they are human and therefore their words and actions are not always graceful – sometimes alarmingly not so – I know because they love me their intentions for me are good. That makes for some very positive intense experiences.

Always remember the people who love you; no matter what, be there for them, and remember we are always here for you. I am always here for you. I cannot tell you what to do, but I will tell you what I'd do.

And even on what I hope is a distant day that I am gone from this earth, know I will be there inside you, to turn to if you need a guide.

I have loosened my hold, and will continue to as you become a man, but I will never let you go.

The Potential People

In addition to nature, in addition to the people who already love me, it is also the strangers who have provided me the most intense experiences.

Never underestimate the positive potential of those you don't yet know.

Everyone who has already influenced the direction of your life – even your parents and grandparents – was once a stranger to you.

Somewhere out there may be your wife. A best friend. Someone who hands you a dream job. Someone whose mentorship helps you live an even happier life.

Some of these people may only enter your life briefly, and the departure of some may bring you temporary heartache, but always remember to recognize what you discovered through them, and be grateful.

Somewhere out there are always more people who can help you positively transform your life. Stay open to meeting them.

The Works

And finally, it is also the great works of strangers that have provided me these intense experiences.

The books, music, films, poetry, plays, comedy performances, paintings, cuisine, engineering feats, architecture, gardens and all the other works of art and passion.

I realize that school, in its admirable attempt to break these works down for study, can sometimes seem to threaten to break their beauty and transformational potential in the process.

But remember that, while it can be necessary and even fascinating to understand the technical components that make up these works, they were created first and foremost from the heart. They were created from someone's desire to put their experience with the world out there for the world.

They may be worthy of study, but they were created for you to experience them ... delve into them and let them move you, let them also be your catalysts and guides.

And so nature, the people who love and care about you, the people you don't yet know, and the great works of people through the ages ... along with your formal studies, your work, exercise and healthy eating, and nurturing your spirituality and faith however you choose ... these are worth your time and energy. No matter what your age, these are experiences that will help you grow constantly and become who you are.

The Deadly Imposters

Meanwhile, beware of the deadly imposters: alcohol, drugs, smoking, gambling, materialism and excessive shopping, brainless TV, heartless sex, fast and processed food, and other reckless behavior like dangerous driving.

These are all severely dangerous narcotics, empty illusions that may seem to momentarily caress your ego even as they slowly and subtly – or sometimes not so slowly and subtly – shred your being to pieces.

These are what kills bodies, brains, hearts, spirit and potential.

Maintain control over these deadly imposters vigilantly. Avoid them is my ideal advice; the more you do, the stronger, happier and better a person you will be. The less you avoid them, the weaker, unhappier and more distant from yourself you will be. There are no two ways about it.

If and where you will dabble in them – and yes, while I myself have done some of them, one of the key marks of maturity is that you don't give yourself permission to repeat others' foolish mistakes, even dear old dad's – maintain the utmost self-discipline and self-honesty.

They are not good to you, they are not good for you, and the moment you find any part of yourself believing any of them are is the moment you must clamp down on them with all your heart and energy.

Your Choices

It is your life; do not allow the sinister lure of anything, and do not allow anyone else's choices, to live it for you.

You are not merely graduating from high school. You are graduating into adulthood. What that means is that you are responsible for your choices.

You are the choices that you make.

Choose positive intense experiences that nurture you. Choose to recognize failings for what they are: necessary building blocks to success. Choose honesty, including unyielding self-honesty, and self-discipline. Choose love, which always starts and ends with self-love.

Choose wisely, son.

I love you,
Dad

*A very Special Acknowledgment to Brian Vaszily.

Brian Vaszily (pronounced "vay zlee") is the founder and editor in chief of IntenseExperiences.com, one of the world's most popular and respected personal growth and wellness websites. Brian Vaszily is also bestselling author, widely renowned and respected life coach, business coach and speaker, and a positive change advocate who has been featured extensively in the media, including ABC, NBC, and Fox News.

ABOUT THE AUTHOR

ABOUT KYTKA "KIT" HILMAR-JEZEK

Truly a radical pioneer in parenting and a mover and shaker in life, Kytka "Kit" Hilmar-Jezek is also known as the founder of Waldorf Homeschoolers. Her first book, Reiki for Children, was self-published in 2003. She has received accolades from Reiki Healers from all over the globe for finally presenting the concept of Reiki to Children. She is also recognized in the Alternative Educational Community as a speaker on children's rights in terms of education.

Through Kit's positive philosophy and outspoken views on parenting techniques, hundreds have learned how to create more of what they want in their family lives. Kit also brings inspiration to bring wellness into their bodies, minds, and spirits.

Kytka has written for various parenting and wellness magazines and her articles and strong opinions have appeared online. She has received awards for her contributions and thousands of letters of support for her strength, speaking and initiatives. The Education Revolution named her into their Hall of Fame. She launched the ReikiKids website and wrote the book Reiki For Children.

Studying with The Universal Life Church she became an Ordained Minister, Reverend, S.O.U.L. Clinic Counselor and Doctor of Philosophy in Religion. Because of her own spiritual intuitions, she also took her family from a vegetarian, to vegan to 100% Living/Raw Foods diet. She recorded her DVD "Raising Kids Raw." She became a Reiki Master and an Honorary Mayan Shaman.

Her children, having been immersed in all of these alternative methods and views each have their own strong sense of identity and connection of body – mind – spirit. Out of these experiences her son Zachary Alexander Jezek's first book, written at age 10 called "My Journey To Becoming a Mayan Shaman" was born. With Kits help & support, he now has several websites including Young Shaman, Tap Into Teen Power, Teen Success Builder and NLP Depot. Following suit, her two daughters Zynnia & Zanna have their own blog as well, called Sisters To Success.

At the threshold of having 25+ years of experience and travel, of profound personal transformation and spiritual journey – her greatest strength is in stepping up onto the podium and speaking of her purpose and the importance of her message. Kytka inspires people to look within for their own strengths and to bring balance into their own lives.

The idea of writing the Age of Attraction came to her as a combination of living in the Age of Aquarius, on the cusp of great global changes, 2012 prophecies, cosmic convergences and the like and the popularity and hyper speed growth of quantum physics and the Law of Attraction.

Kit is an incredible woman. She has created incredible abundance in her own life, many times over. She laughs as she shares that she had to do it many times over just to allow it to fall away to remind herself of the Buddhist principles of attachment. To let all of the "stuff" go. She has always been a tireless and hands-on worker in all of the various themes she delved into. She has utilized herself and her children and living examples of the principles she believes in and people who know her personally all share her best attribute – she has always walked her talk. More importantly – she has always and unrelentingly always remained true to her soul purpose.

Her wealth and abundance of the gifted people, the teachers and healers and incredible minds she has interacted with and met along her journey has been a direct result of actively practicing the Law of Attraction and manifesting these great Mentors into her life. A Lifelong lover of learning, she has read over 10,000 books and attended over $100,000 in seminars, often as a guest of the speaker who loves to hear her insight and values her generous recommendations if she believes in what they do.

Kit continuously strives to lead people to new realms of thinking about health, wealth, relationships, a peaceful world and living abundantly and with all of the wonderful power that lies within their most glorious authentic selves. She conveys this with intelligence, humor, facts, personal sharing and baring and a sense of humor and wit. Her goal and passion is to attract the right partners to assist her with putting out into the world all she has gathered from the garden of her own life. She is a serious multi-tasker who sleeps only 4 hours a night and tells you she runs on the high octane of LIFE!

Kytka is the proud mother of 3 beautiful home-birthed, wise, remarkable, empathetic and spiritual children. She attributes a large part of her dynamic ability as an author, speaker and coach and her mastery in her own life, to her experience as a parent who chose to parent from the heart and be an individual versus a part of any group, which we as social beings often prefer.

Learn more about Kytka and her children at:

www.FamilyHealingSeries.com

AFTERWARD

I wanted to share my enthusiasm and healing benefits of Reiki with my own children, so I began to look for information geared specifically towards children regarding Reiki. No matter where I looked, I came up empty handed. Informative sources were very few and far between and no one seemed to have anything worthwhile to contribute.

As a writer and editor of several publications, I began making notes, organizing them into a format and suddenly the conception of a Children's Reiki class manual had taken place.

A few months later, this book was born. This book was originally designed as a "class manual" which I had intended to offer along with Reiki Level One and Two Attunements and Certificates for children. I later decided that all of this wonderful information would serve more standing on it's own and being available to a broader audience, hence the birth of the book.

In closing, I would you to think about how wonderful a world we live in, where you may pick up a book and teach yourself all you need to know, about anything that interests you. You have the power to create a future for yourself where your actions will be used in a positive way and will touch the lives of many others. Be responsible and live by the Reiki Principles daily, even if you never practice Reiki.

Our time is one where we truly live in a global village and we are lucky enough to be able to meet with all kinds of people from many different walks of life. We also share this wonderful earth with all sorts of other living beings. Many we do not understand. Many we do not and will not ever know, but all of who deserve the wonderful power of love, healing and loving kindness.

Now, I would like to take you full circle back to the beginning:

Who has the healing touch?

You do!

You were born with incredible healing power.

Yes, you were.

It is a gift to you from the Mother Father Creator of All.

You were born out of Love.

You were born out of Light.

People call this very special and strong love Universal Life Force.

This powerful energy stays with you your whole life.

With this energy you can do anything you hope to do.

With practice, you can use this energy to heal

You already are a Reiki Healer!

BIBLIOGRAPHY

Reiki: A Torch in Daylight
by Karyn Mitchell

Essential Reiki: A Complete Guide to an Ancient Healing Art.
by Diane Stein

Modern Reiki Method for Healing
by Hiroshi Doi

The Power of Reiki
by Tanmaya Honervogt

The Spirit of Reiki
by Walter Lubeck, Frank Arjava Petter & William Lee Rand.

The Original Reiki Handbook of Dr Mikao Usui
by Frank Arjava Petter

Hands of Light: A Guide to Healing Through the Human Energy Field
by Barbara Ann Brennan

Mayan Reiki I and Mayan Reiki II
by Reverend Dennis Alexander, Ph.D.

The Book on Karuna Reiki: Advanced Healing Energy for Our Evolving World
by Laurelle Shanti Gaia

You Can See Auras
by Wendy Lampert

For a complete listing of all of the books in our Family Healing Series, please visit the website at:

www.FamilyHealingSeries.com

NOTES

NOTES

NOTES

NOTES

NOTES

NOTES

NOTES

NOTES

NOTES

NOTES

NOTES

NOTES

NOTES

NOTES

Made in the USA
Lexington, KY
21 August 2012